Towards a Structure of Indifference

SOCIOLOGY AND ECONOMICS
Controversy and Integration

An Aldine de Gruyter Series of Texts and Monographs

SERIES EDITORS

Paula S. England, *University of Arizona, Tucson*
George Farkas, *University of Texas, Dallas*
Kevin Lang, *Boston University*

Values in the Marketplace
James Burk

Equal Employment Opportunity:
Labor Market Discrimination and Public Policy
Paul Burstein (ed.)

Industries, Firms, and Jobs
Sociological and Economic Approaches
[Expanded Edition]
George Farkas and Paula England (eds.)

Towards a Structure of Indifference
The Social Origins of Maternal Custody
Debra Friedman

Beyond the Marketplace:
Rethinking Economy and Society
Roger Friedland and A. F. Robertson (eds.)

Social Institutions:
Their Emergence, Maintenance and Effects
Michael Hechter, Karl-Dieter Opp and Reinhard Wippler (eds.)

The Origin of Values
Michael Hechter, Lynn Nadel and Richard E. Michod (eds.)

Parents' Jobs and Children's Lives
Toby L. Parcel and Elizabeth G. Menaghan

Power, Norms, and Inflation: A Skeptical Treatment
Michael R. Smith

Towards a Structure of Indifference

The Social Origins of Maternal Custody

DEBRA FRIEDMAN

ALDINE DE GRUYTER
New York

About the Author

Debra Friedman is Assistant Dean of Undergraduate Education, University of Washington. She is a frequent contributor to major professional journals on the subjects of theory, social order, and the value of children.

ALDINE DE GRUYTER
A division of Walter de Gruyter, Inc.
200 Saw Mill River Road
Hawthorne, New York 10532

This publication is printed on acid free paper ⊚

Library of Congress Cataloging-in-Publication Data

Friedman, Debra, 1955–
    Towards a structure of indifference : the social origins of
maternal custody / Debra Friedman.
        p. cm. — (Sociology and economics)
    Includes bibliographical references and index.
    ISBN 0-202-30495-7 (alk. paper). — ISBN 0-202-30496-5 (pbk.
alk. paper)
    1. Children of divorced parents. 2. Custody of children.
3. Parent and child. I. Title. II. Series.
HQ777.5.F75 1994
306.89—dc20   94-22613
                                                                CIP

Manufactured in the United States of America

10 9 8 7 6 5 4 3 2 1

For Michael, for whom all things matter

The opposite of love is not hate, it's indifference.
—Elie Wiesel, 1986

The tragedy of love is indifference.
—W. Somerset Maugham, 1921

Contents

Acknowledgments

In the famous story of the emperor who wore no clothes, it is the child alone who speaks the truth, the child alone who sees the true condition of the emperor. Not only do the adults fail to speak the truth but they do not see it, for their vision is obscured by the force of norms. Even more than this, the adults wish their emperor to be cloaked in splendor, and this wish is strong enough to make it appear so in their eyes.

Children do not speak on their own behalf in matters of divorce and custody. When we write on their behalf we do so in ways that do not include them. Those of us who were children of divorce write as adults. More often, those of us who write of divorce are married and divorced. We write without fear of the judgments of the small voices who are our subjects. Since they are not present in our debates, children cannot say whether our laws, arguments, and judgments are truly splendiferous, or merely the invisible threads of well-meaning social constructions.

To think about developing arguments that might withstand the evaluation of children still able to discern truth from falsehood is a luxury impossible in the normal routines of academic life. I was extremely fortunate to have three opportunities to work at places removed from these routines. The first opportunity was provided by the Russell Sage Foundation where I was a Visiting Scholar during the 1988–1989 academic year. It was there that this project was conceived and first presented to a group of distinguished scholars including sociologists, historians, psychologists, and economists. Had I been able to address all of their questions, this book would have been better than it is. As it is, the book was shaped by their interests, encouragement, and criticisms.

One year passed before I returned to work on the book at the Hoover Institution at Stanford University where I was one of the 1990–1991 National Fellows. The book was written there. Hoover provided the best conditions I have ever experienced for scholarship, not only because of the time it offered but also because of its intellectual environment. Presenting one's work before the Senior and National Fellows of the Domestic Studies group at Hoover, composed principally of economists and political scientists, can be an electrifying experience. The importance placed on policy at Hoover by scholars of widely differing political orientations compels everyone to ask one question of their work: what's the point? Special thanks go to Raquel Fernandez and Barry Weingast for their contributions to my intellectual development.

The prospect of returning to routine academic life situated in a single discipline and without concern for policy was depressing. The Udall Center for Studies in Public Policy at the University of Arizona offered me an alternative to this scenario, and I became a Visiting Fellow there for the 1991–1992 academic year. The Udall Center houses a small group of interdisciplinary faculty interested in developing the policy implications of their research, including philosophers, political scientists, and sociologists drawn principally from the local faculty. Following that year, I was invited to stay on—indefinitely, as it turned out—as a Visiting Scholar. I revised the book several times while in residence. Although I continued to teach in the Department of Sociology, the Udall Center provided a scholarly home. My gratitude to the Director, Helen Ingram, and the Associate Director, Bob Varady is immense.

Several groups have played a role in the formulation of the book. Seminars held at New York University, Northwestern University, the University of Adelaide, and the University of Arizona raised important issues. A summer spent at the Australian National University as a Visiting Scholar in the Sociology group at the Research School for the Social Sciences broadened my sense of the international importance of child custody dilemmas.

Fred Campbell, Paula England, Michael Hechter, Doug McAdam, and Kathleen Schwartzman all read the manuscript from start to finish. Each offered something invaluable. Doug McAdam and Kathleen Schwartzman paid special attention to the empirical inadequacies of the book and suggested ways to address them. Paula England—who eventually became a sponsor of the book as co-editor of the series in which it is published —lived up to her reputation as being one of the toughest and most constructive editors around. Michael Hechter not only ruthlessly examined each step of the theoretical argument but suggested ways to address the problems. When I was awash in criticisms from all directions, Fred Campbell restored my spirit by reminding me that the purpose was to write what was authentic, and evaluated the manuscript in that light. Many of the most trenchant criticisms of the manuscript—ones that caused me to fundamentally rethink the argument—were offered by people whose names I do not know, but to whom I am nonetheless grateful. Among the parade of research assistants who contributed to the labor of this book in one way or another special thanks go to Carol Diem. My brother, Spencer Thal, provided invaluable legal research assistance and general encouragement. Among this list of people are my friends—a list to which Nancy Durbin and Mindy Fain must be added—who were there during the times of pleasure and despair. Special appreciation goes to my father Paul Friedman for his tenaciousness in parenting, as in all things.

My daughter Eliana bore the brunt of the time I invested in the project. She cannot know how important her voice was to me. I listened hard to her fears as her friends' parents began to divorce. I basked in her unexpected encouragement. I drew on her considerable empathy, intuition, and analytic skill to discuss many of the issues in this book, particularly those in the last chapter. She despises the epigram of this book, but that is because she has known only love and hate. I hope that is always so.

1

Divorce and the Social Bargain: Child Custody in Historical Context

At a dinner party held in England sometime during the 1890s, Henry James was told of an unusual court settlement in a divorce case: instead of being awarded to the father or to the mother, the child was committed by the judge to spend portions of time with each parent. Subsequently, James heard that the child displeased its new stepparent, and so was unwelcome in at least one home. This state of affairs sparked James' imagination:

> The accidental mention had been made to me of the manner in which the situation of some luckless child of a divorced couple was affected, under my informant's eyes, by the remarriage of one of its parents—I forget which; so that, thanks to the limited desire for its company expressed by the step-parent, the law of its little life, its being entertained in rotation by its father and its mother, wouldn't easily prevail. Whereas each of these persons had at first vindictively desired to keep it from the other, so at present the remarried relative sought now rather to be rid of it—that is to leave it as much as possible, and beyond the appointed times and seasons, on the hand of the adversary; which malpractice, resented by the latter as bad faith, would of course be repaid and avenged by an equal treachery. The wretched infant was thus to find itself practically disowned, rebounding from racquet to racquet like a tennis ball or shuttlecock. (James 1897, p. 23)

The character of Maisie emerged from this story. In his book, *What Maisie Knew*, the girl finds herself in a circumstance similar to the "luckless" child mentioned to James, but with a twist interesting to the issue of child custody. Maisie ends up as a "shuttlecock" just as the child he heard about did, but in the book—and much truer to history—Maisie's misfortunes were brought about more by parental than by court design. The court awarded custody of Maisie to her father, as was the norm in that period, although this seemed like a choice between lesser evils:

1

The litigation had seemed interminable and had in fact been complicated; but by the decision on the appeal the judgement of the divorce-court was confirmed as to the assignment of the child. The father, who, though bespattered from head to foot, had made good his case, was, in pursuance of this triumph, appointed to keep her: it was not so much that the mother's character had been more absolutely damaged as that the brilliancy of a lady's complexion (and this lady's, in court, was immensely remarked) might be regarded as showing more the spots. (James 1897, p. 35)

Yet with the aid of their lawyers, the parents quickly circumvented the court order to make arrangements more to their liking:

Attached, however, to the second pronouncement was a condition that detracted, for Beale Farange, from its sweetness—an order that he should refund to his late wife the twenty-six hundred pounds put down by her, as it was called, some three years before, in the interest of the child's maintenance and precisely on a proved understanding that he would take no proceedings: a sum of which he had had the administration and of which he could render not the least account. The obligation thus attributed to her adversary was no small balm to Ida's resentment; it drew a part of the sting from her defeat and compelled Mr. Farange perceptibly to lower his crest. He was unable to produce the money or to raise it in any way; so that after a squabble scarcely less public and scarcely more decent than the original shock of battle his only issue from his predicament was a compromise proposed by his legal advisers and finally accepted by hers. (James 1897, p. 35)

What was left with which to bargain? The child, of course:

His debt was by this arrangement remitted to him and the little girl disposed of in a manner worthy of the judgement-seat of Solomon. She was divided in two and the portions tossed impartially to the disputants. They would take her, in rotation, for six months at a time; she would spend half the year with each. (James 1897, p. 35)

In this opening scene, James has captured the complex relation between law, judicial decision, parents' interests, and children's welfare, both historically specific lessons and those that go beyond a single time or place. The decision of the court to award Maisie to her father reflects the times: English courts in the 1890s would be expected to prefer fathers, particularly elite ones. Sometimes mothers were able to mount effective countercases, although the questionable morality of the mother would have weighed against her more heavily than did the questionable morality of the father. Why English courts preferred fathers in the late 1800s, as did most courts in Western countries in this time period, and why courts came to prefer mothers by the early twentieth century are key questions that I shall address.

Yet prior to the question of this historically specific change in court preferences are the deeper issues on which James touches. What is striking about Maisie is how much she mattered in the contest between her two parents, but how little her own well-being mattered to them. Her profound importance in the divorce proceedings and their aftermath cannot be overestimated, yet this cannot be mistaken for her parents' concern for her. It is possible for parents—and courts—to conceive of and execute custody arrangements in the name of the child, behind the rhetoric of the child's interests, but with little consideration for the child's interests. James saw with clarity what most modern observers and critics of child custody arrangements cannot or will not see: that parents have interests separable from those of their children and that they can be expected to act on these interests. In Maisie's case, the allocation of her presence between her parents could be bartered for a mutually agreeable financial settlement.

James wrote from Maisie's point of view. This distinguishes his book from nearly all other books on child custody, fictional or historical, legal or sociological. His purpose was to lay bare the truths of divorce for one child and one man and one woman in relation to that child. Had he written, instead, from the woman's point of view, he might have celebrated her liberation from an unfortunate marriage, her triumph in getting her way despite the paternalist limitations of the court, her freedom to forge a new relationship and a new life. He wrote, instead, of the child's bewilderment and pain, and of the actions of the adults as they were expressed through the child's life.

I, too, adopt a child-centric stance. My purpose is different, though, than James'. Mine is to try to understand the deeper structural causes and consequences of contemporary child custody arrangements. Much has been written about the advantages and disadvantages of divorce for women and men. There is also a large empirical literature that attempts to assess the effects of various custody arrangements on the developmental outcomes of children. I want to broaden that discussion by looking at the structural design of divorce and custody arrangements and asking not whether children fare better or worse if they are in intact families or divorced ones, but whether they are advantaged or disadvantaged by the laws, norms, and institutions that permit their parents to divorce and make custodial arrangements on their behalf. *Purpose of the Book?*

In this discussion, I will rely on Elinor Ostrom's definitions of institutions and rules. Institutions are, for her, "sets of working rules that are used to determine who is eligible to make decisions in some arena, what actions are allowed or constrained, what aggregations rules will be used, what procedures must be followed, what information must or must not be provided, and what payoffs will be assigned to individuals dependent on their actions" (Ostrom 1990, p. 51). This is a particularly useful dynamic definition of institutions since in the area of child custody variations and changes in practice—in working rules—are common. Working rules are defined as those rules "actually used, monitored, and enforced when individuals make choices about the actions they will take" (Ostrom 1990, p. 51), and they may or may not be coincident with formal laws.

Because working rules may have many sources, and because the subject matter of child custody is itself complex, the task of uncovering the logic of institutional design is a challenge. For every instance of a child custody arrangement gone awry, there is another that is working adequately. Some custodial mothers receive child-support payments (on time and in full); many others do not. Some noncustodial fathers are satisfied with their level of involvement in their children's lives; many others are not. Some judges feel that the area of custody determination is a legal and ethical morass; others feel that they are competent to make determinations. Some psychologists and psychiatrists believe that children's emotional development is not necessarily hindered by divorce; others find cause for concern. There are good mothers and bad mothers, good fathers and bad fathers, wise judicial decisions and foolish ones.

If someone were designing a set of domestic arrangements that really took the interests of the children as paramount, would the current congeries of laws, precedents, judgments, and private arrangements that comprise the fate of children of divorce be the result? What constitutes the best interests of the child following divorce is hardly self-evident. What criteria are proper for judging: Is the key the celerity of the award, the stability of the parent, the material resources available to children, the closeness of the present parent–child relationship, prior parental investment in the child, the avoidance of conflict, or the appearance of fairness? In what hierarchical order should these and other considerations be taken into account if they produce inconsistent or even conflicting outcomes?

Where does the confusion that characterizes child custody institutions come from? Is it merely from the great variety in social conditions? Certainly families—both intact and divorced ones—function at widely different levels of social, emotional, and financial well-being. Does the confusion come from our inability to identify the true preferences and needs of children and their parents? Social scientists have long wished to be able to reach into the interior landscapes of individuals to determine their true preferences; if they could, custody decisions might well become a great deal less ambiguous.

Yet part of the confusion, I believe, comes from an inadequate understanding of the parent–child relation both within the intact family and the divorced one, as well as an inadequate understanding of the relationship between the family and the state. There is a fundamental *structural* difference between the parent–child relation in an intact family and in a divorced one that has important consequences for the relationship between the family and the state.

The Parent–Child Relation

A child is a jointly produced collective good (Weiss and Willis 1985).[1] The nature of the child's joint production is obvious, but it may result from a carefully considered collective decision of a wife and husband to an unplanned event. A collective good—a child or any other—is defined principally by the infeasibility of exclusion (Hardin 1982).[2] One can enjoy the good regardless of whether one has contributed to it.

As with other collective goods, children require continuing contributions: nurture, material resources, and education, which translate into day-to-day investments of one or more adults. In behavioral terms, nurture is translated into responding to the child's cries in the night, changing diapers, feeding, playing games with and reading to the child, and a host of other unremitting tasks. Some of these tasks are pleasurable, others are not; nearly all of them must be done at the child's behest rather than at the parent's pleasure. Material investments are likewise continuous, but more indirect. The child requires food, shelter, and clothing every day, every week, every month, and every year; the needs do not abate and may increase over time. These are usually provided by one or both parents' paid labor outside of the home.

In an intact family with two parents, each parent makes contributions to the child. These contributions are by no means necessarily equal. Mothers ordinarily contribute more to the behaviors associated with nurture, even if they work outside the home. Fathers ordinarily contribute more to material support. The child requires both kinds of contributions for his or her well-being.

Yet if the child is a collective good, why don't the parents free ride? Instead of concerted efforts of both parents to spend time with their children, feed and clothe them, attend to their school work, why don't we observe each parent sitting by while the other parent does all? After all, they are able to enjoy the child's accomplishments and affections even if they do not contribute to the child's well-being. There are two, interconnected reasons. Were the parents both to free ride, there would be little in the way of accomplishments or affections for them to enjoy:

the child would wither in the absence of parental investments. But the more important reason theoretically is that the parents exert social control over one another in the context of the family: each attempts to ensure that the other contributes his or her fair share (however they happen to decide what this share consists of).

Social control is made possible by the strong affective ties of the members of the family, as well as by economies in monitoring and sanctioning that come from the small size of families and their common knowledge base (Hechter 1987). In the context of a family, mothers and fathers monitor (and sanction) each other's contributions to the child. They may do so in the context of a shared standard of fairness (what constitutes an appropriate contribution to the child), or they may have different standards. The degree to which each is successful in compelling the other to contribute according to a personally defined standard will depend upon their degree of power and dependence on the other (Emerson 1962). Power-dependence relations are rarely static; as they change, so will the level of each member's contribution to the child.

It is important to note that children have little power to compel their parent's contribution to their welfare. One can think of many situations in which children have intense wants, particularly for parental time and attention, in which they are powerless to bring about the desired outcome. They may have needs of which they are unaware, such as the need for special schooling or tutoring, in the case of giftedness or learning disability. They may have conscious wants for a great variety of material goods, as well, which they are denied because the parent has decided to expend always-scarce resources elsewhere. Their powerlessness comes not from the lack of an emotional bond, but rather from *the absence of alternative sources of gratification* of their needs and wants, at least until they reach school and/or a reasonable degree of autonomy of action.

Thus, in intact families, parents contribute to their children rather than free riding because each parent exerts control over the other. This control need not be draconian: it may come in the form of encouragement and esteem given to each other (positive sanctioning) for their unique contribution to the child's well being.

In contrast, in divorced families, the child remains a collective good, *but each parent's incentive to contribute to the child is diminished by the absence of the other parent.* None of the social control mechanisms that operate to encourage contribution in intact families exists any longer. On this basis alone, there will be suboptimal contributions to the child, in the absence of third-party enforcement.

The primary example of the suboptimal contribution to the child is the failure of noncustodial fathers to provide child support. From the theoretical standpoint advanced here, this failure should be no surprise. Remember that contribution to the child depends not on the love each parent feels toward the child but on the control each parent exerts over the other's behavior to prevent free riding. Once the family is no longer an intact group, such endogenous social control mechanisms are rapidly attenuated.

Custodial mothers may also reduce their contributions to the child for the same reason that noncustodial fathers do. Their reductions are likely to be far more subtle and harder to capture empirically. Remarriage—involving time spent dating and courting, investing in another who has no incentive to contribute to the child, and having more children with the new spouse—all direct the mother's attention, time, and resources away from the child of the first marriage. The statistic that tells us that half of stepparents do not even count their stepchildren as part of their close family (Regan 1993, p. 56) suggests that many stepparents do not feel bound to encourage optimal levels of contribution to children from previous marriages. Thus a reconstituted family does not usually take the place of the original one from the point of view of the child.[3]

There are two ways to circumvent the problem of suboptimal contributions to collective goods in the absence of endogenous social control. The first is through third-party enforcement. Clearly that is the intent behind programs to get the government to act as an enforcer to recover child support payments from dads. There are two drawbacks with such programs, however. First, third-party enforcement is expensive, and the cost is borne by others (taxpayers), though the claim is usually made that the alternative—some form of social welfare payments—is even more expensive (to taxpayers). Nonetheless, it is a far more expensive alternative to the cost of social control borne by the intact family. Second, third-party enforcement rarely can produce an optimal level of contribution. The costs of gathering information specific to each case simply would be too great. Note that this informational cost is also close to zero in the intact family, in contrast to the fragmented one.

The second way to circumvent the problem of suboptimal contributions is to privatize the good. Private goods are excludable, unlike collective ones. If the custodial parent, then, can find a way to privatize the child—to alienate, in the strictest sense, the noncustodial parent from the child and successfully keep him from enjoying the benefits of the child's company, affection, and achievements—then the child is no longer a collective good, and therefore is not subject to incentives for free riding. If custodial parents were to behave in a purely instrumental fashion, we would expect them to seek to privatize the child in just this manner *and* simultaneously get the noncustodial parent to continue to make a financial contribution.

The implications of the contrast between intact and divorced family structure for the child's well being therefore are profound. While suboptimal contributions to the child *may* occur in an intact family due to insufficient social control, they are almost *certain* to occur in the divorced family because of the attenuation of any endogenous social control. Neither in the intact nor in the divorced family does the child have a means by which to compel contributions to his or her well being.

Not only are children powerless to secure optimal levels of parental investment, particularly in divorced families, but they are also unable to ensure that parents adequately represent their interests *when those interests conflict with the parents' interests*.

The child is a whole being, separate from the adult. Parents, acting as agents on behalf of their children, may or may not heed those interests. There are numerous scenarios in which we can imagine why parents should not heed those interests. Children may have an indefensible preference for their short-term as against their long-term interests. Children may be unable to assess the full range of consequences of any given desired behavior. Children may place unrealistically small weights on safety considerations. The advantaged position of parents to make decisions on behalf of their children comes from these asymmetries of knowledge, maturity, and competence.

These asymmetries are insufficient, however, to support a claim that the interests of parents can somehow stand in for the interests of their children. In fact, these asymmetries mean that there is significant potential for divergence of interests between parents and children. The divergence of interests gives rise to a classic principal–agent situation.[4]

In all such situations an agent is one who is empowered to act on behalf of a principal. Principals usually empower agents; in the case of parent–child relations, however, it is the state that empowers parents to act as agents on behalf of children. In most principal–agent relations, the principal bears ultimate responsibility to honor obligations incurred by agents. In the case of children and their parents, it is children who bear the ultimate burden of the decisions and investments made on their behalf.

In no arena are principals and agents substitutable. This is because agents often have interests different than those of the principals they represent. In such situations it is axiomatic that agents will pursue courses of action that diverge from those that principals would have pursued had they been acting on their own behalf. There is here a significant agency risk: a risk that the agents, the parents, will use their superior knowledge and capability to pursue their own interests at the expense of the principals, the children.

Since the divergence of interests is a given in all principal–agent relations, the issue always hinges on the sorts of constraints the principals can place on the agents' behavior to keep them from taking courses of action prompted by their own, separable, interests. The key question here is what stops parents from pursuing their own interests when they are at odds with or detrimental to the interests of their children. To reiterate, other than persuasion or threat, children have little recourse to constrain their parents' behavior. The state, which empowers parents as agents, also has few realistic means to constrain behavior, and does so only for the most flagrant violations of children's interests (when parents harm their children, for instance, and sometimes not even then).

This source of risk to children is insidious: if children are unable to make arguments on their own behalf, they must rely on their parents to do so. But parents, because of their separable interests, are unlikely to weigh the relative merits of the competing positions of their children and themselves. Most parents have a well-developed repertoire of explanations for their actions—nowhere more evident than when they decide to divorce—with which children cannot hope to compete. They have neither the capacity to make equally finessed arguments nor the resources to be heard if they could.

Children's greatest hope, then, would have to be that their interests do not often diverge from those of their parents. Another way to think of this is that since neither children nor the state have the social control resources to constrain parents, children are likely to be better off when they live in a situation in which it is in their parents' interests to provide for their basic needs and wants, particularly for nurture, material support, and education. This conclusion has implications similar to the one above: children are better off in intact families than in divorced ones, in this instance because their interests are less likely to conflict with those of their parents.

Risks to children come both from their parents' suboptimal contributions and from their separable interests. These are problems of all families, but are more pronounced in divorced families. At the same time that the family is a source of considerable risk for children, it is also the primary risk-reducing institution for children.

The Family as a Risk-Reducing Institution

Nearly all social institutions have at their root some risk-reducing function, no more so than the family. The family provides social insur-

ance for adults and children for a wide range of present and future
uncertainties. The members of a family have different levels of need for
material support, affection, and support during times of illness, but the
importance of the family is that it responds to the changing needs of its
members over the life course. Adults may find themselves temporarily
without a job, or may face a period of extended ill-health. These vicissitudes of life are unforeseeable, for the most part, and the family ensures
that its individual members do not have to self-insure for every conceiv-
able ill-wind. On a daily basis, the family provides emotional support, a
haven in a heartless world (Lasch 1983). Increasingly, adults are able
to find alternatives to their families as risk-reducing institutions. The
state provides unemployment insurance for those who lose their jobs,
welfare for those who cannot provide for themselves, and a modicum of
health benefits for the seriously ill.

But an equally important alternative to a present family is a future
family. For a man or woman, one family is essentially substitutable with
the next. Thus, if an individual finds his or her marriage unsuitable in
some way, relatively uncomplicated divorce and marriage laws will permit that individual to leave one marriage and contract for the next. An
individual may do better or worse in the choice of a spouse from the
point of view of the spouse's willingness to engage in risk pooling, but
since it is the family itself that is the risk-reducing institution, this function does not depend entirely on individual propensities. Additionally,
future uncertainties that face all individuals make an especially good
basis on which to expect social exchange.

The situation for children is strikingly different from that of their
parents. Whereas adults can constitute and reconstitute families that
serve their needs, there is no sense in which families are substitutable
for children. There are alternative sources of risk-reduction for
children—including state-provided benefits, as for adults—but these
require their parents to act on their behalf as agents to obtain and distrib-
ute them.

There are several reasons for the asymmetry. During the course of
childhood, children typically contribute only affection—but not material
resources—to the risk pool. If parents are motivated by the possibility of
future leveling of the exchange with their children, they are much more
likely to be confident of the biological child's willingness to repay at a
later date, than of the stepchild's. This may be due in part to the different levels of altruism that have their basis in genes, but there is another
source: most stepchildren have alternatives to their stepparents (that is,
their biological parents), and so their future loyalty is much more in
question.

Additionally, as I argued above, the stepparent has fewer incentives to contribute to the child than does the biological or adoptive parent, but, more importantly, the child's mother or father also has fewer incentives to contribute to their child outside of the original nuclear family.

Analysis of other social insurance groups (Hechter 1987)—rotating credit associations, friendly societies, and primordial groups of all sorts—suggests another reason for the asymmetry. These groups depend on continuing participation of their members and on social conditions that preclude the possibility that one member can abscond with the group's pooled resources. Thus, the members of such groups cannot be differentially dependent on the group to any large degree, for this will threaten the group's future.

Yet differential dependence precisely describes the asymmetry of children and adults with respect to any given family. Children are highly dependent and do not have the wits or the force of law to take the group's resources and move on. But adults do, and when they divorce, they destroy the pool from which the child's well-being has previously been provided.

Divorce and the Social Bargain

Bearing and raising children often seem like a private matter, yet parents raise children by leave of the state. This is difficult to observe in everyday life, and easier to see when parents violate the social bargain, when, for example, they physically abuse their children in such a way as to call public attention to the abuse. Parental privileges can then be terminated. Parents who have been through divorce and contested custody battles also come to understand intuitively that they parent at the state's discretion. In fact, however, parents now always parent by privilege rather than by right.

The privilege to parent rests on a social bargain: parents raise children unless they divorce or die or engage in behavior that outrages public morality, however defined in the historical moment. Presumably the social bargain rests on some notion that to the extent that children are a society's next generation of citizens, society gets significant benefits from having parents raise their children rather than other agents.

Because the notion that parenting results from a social bargain rather than flowing from a biological reality is difficult to countenance, it may be important to remember that components of parental privilege have been revoked in the past. Compulsory schooling is one such example. The obligation to provide education was once the handmaiden of paternal rights. Now, the quantity and quality of education are discretionary only for those parents of significant means or intense beliefs combined with boundless time, and then only within state-issued regulations.

A purely economic analysis of the social bargain might conclude that the bargain was the most efficient means of providing successive generations of worthy societal members. Yet even if such an analysis did yield this sort of result, it would necessarily rest on a host of assumptions about parents as decision makers. In other words, in order to model the actions of parents, *as distinct from other actors*, the model would have to include assumptions referring to the special motivations of parents.

There are at least four such assumptions upon which the special status of parents rests. The first is that parents are more altruistic toward their children than others would be. The claim seems to have validity: parents choose to have their children, love them, share genes with them, get psychic benefits from raising them well, and so on. Further, parents' attachment to their children often seems difficult to explain on instrumental grounds alone.

The second assumption is that parents have an intrinsic motivation to see that their children attain their highest potential. Parents seem to want their children to achieve well in school, in marriage, and in their jobs, not so much because they benefit directly, but rather because they desire the best for their offspring. Parents are considered more likely than others to work for the most advantageous future for their children.

The third assumption is that parents will exercise adequate self-regulation. Because they are altruistically motivated and anxious to ensure positive outcomes for their children, they will provide a maximum amount of emotional and financial support and encouragement necessary for their children to attain these ends. Their decisions regarding the proper balance of their own needs and wants as against those of their children are assumed to be defensible. Connected with this third assumption is a fourth: that parents should enjoy substantial freedom from external regulation and significant autonomy in the upbringing of their children.

Are these assumptions warranted? There are both theoretical and empirical reasons to suggest reconsideration. Some of the theoretical reasons have already been discussed. Regular and continuing altruism toward children—actions consistent with altruistic motivations—is a by-product of family structure, not an impulse that rests within the hearts of parents, and it is consistent with an intact family structure that allows for endogenous control mechanism.

The self-regulation assumption is also problematic. An agent is the *least* obvious candidate for regulator when regulation is necessary. The authority for self-regulation far better serves the interests of the parents than it does the interests of the children. When the agent diverges from the interests of the principal on the grounds of his or her own self-interest, as is possible whenever their interests diverge, there is no incentive for the agent to forego those interests in favor of the principal's. In an intact family there is at least the minimal regulation afforded by the existence of two adults, each watchful over the other's actions. It is possible, of course, that they will take a stance as a corporate body with respect to the child's interests, but it is also possible that they will control one another's less considerate impulses with respect to the child. In an intact family, there is the possibility that one of the child's parents will act as an agent-turned-advocate. In a divorced family, that is much less probable: there is only one parent (agent) in the household, and when the parent's and the child's interests diverge, the child has no possible recourse. Yet it is important to note that the self-regulation assumption is weak even in the intact family.

The putative justification for according parents special status comes from a social bargain. In exchange for certain social benefits, including exceptionally altruistic behavior and cost-effective self-regulation on the part of a group that applies special knowledge on behalf of those lacking this knowledge, the state grants special status, a favored and relatively secure position, and considerable freedom from external regulation. Parent–child relations are socially constructed inequalities whose justification depends on the fairness of the social bargain. Whether this bargain is a good one depends on whether there is convincing evidence that the elevated status and favored position of parents do in fact, support altruism, and whether there is convincing evidence that parents are exercising self-regulation that is superior to other forms of control.

What appears to be self-regulation and altruism, depends, however, on structural arrangements that promote social control. When those structural arrangements begin to break down, so too does self-regulation and altruism in parenting. In the absence of structurally based social control over parents, the continuing belief in parents' special status comes to have serious social costs.

Reconsidering the Social Bargain

It is those social costs that compel reconsideration of the social bargain. Four social processes have contributed to the erosion of the bargain. The rise in the divorce rate over the last century is perhaps the most dramatic. I have remarked on the differences between the structure of intact families and the structure of divorced families from the child's point of view earlier in this chapter. Additionally, divorce rates are the subject of Chapter 4, and so I will not dwell on it here. Suffice it

to say that the prevalence of divorce means that more than half of all children currently live in a structure that does not provide incentives for parents to maximize their investment in their children during childhood. Divorce often precludes intergenerational transfers, as well (Becker 1991).

The second social process that has eroded confidence in the social bargain is the separation of obligations for children among mothers, fathers, and the state. The diffusion of responsibility that has resulted— the structure of indifference—is the subject of this book generally. What it has meant is that no single agent can answer definitively the question posed by Coleman (1990): "Who will take responsibility for the whole child?"

The third process is no less than the transformation in basic social structure. Coleman (1993) argues that when primordial social organization gave way to purposively constructed social organization, the elemental unit of society shifted from the family to the corporate actor. Social control mechanisms changed, as well, from norms, status, and reputation to rules, laws, formal structures, incentives, and sanctions. In the former, the organization of social life emphasized closure in social structure, which allowed individuals to accumulate social capital.

The consequences for childrearing, and therefore for children themselves, are considerable. The care of children increasingly has moved outside of the home, particularly to schools. Yet Coleman (1993, p. 12) cautions:

> Raising a child to be of value to society entails a much richer mix of goals than schools characteristically address. These goals include managing one's own affairs, taking responsibility for others, working in coordination toward collective goals, in brief, all the things entailed in becoming a mature adult. Parents in broken and patched-together families are becoming increasingly incapable of accomplishing these broader goals for their children, and the schools are not well designed to take on these goals.

Connected with this is the last social process, the severing of the link between parents' and children's future welfare (Coleman 1993). This has special consequences for broken or "patched-together" families whose members find that

> carrying the family's honor into the future is less important. One result of these changes is sharply reduced incentives for parents to bring up their children to be productive. There is no reason to expect parents to be motivated to bring up their child to maximize the child's value to society. (Coleman 1993, p. 12)

The increased divorce rate, the separation of obligations for children, the shift away from the family as the basic unit of the society, and separation of parents' future welfare from their children's all mark fundamental structural changes that call into question the social bargain between parents and the societies in which they live. If parents no longer have sufficient incentives to invest in their children's short- and long-term welfare, who does?

The State's Interest in Children's Welfare

Children have an interest in their own welfare, of course, but they have no means by which to provide for themselves, either independently or by compelling others to do so. But states also have an interest in children, not for their own sake, but for both the potential good they can contribute as well as for the harm they are capable of inflicting on others. Coleman (1993, p. 13) notes:

> There is, however, one actor with strong interests in maximizing a child's value to society, or minimizing its cost. This is the state. The costs of undeveloped human capital (and conversely the benefits of its development) accrue to governments: costs of schooling; costs of crime (including the cost of apprehending and incarcerating criminals); costs of welfare payments; medical costs induced by lifestyles; costs associated with alcohol and drug use; and finally, on the other side of the ledger, benefits from income taxes.

When parents fail to provide maximally so that the child's highest potential is reached, the state loses. When parents fail to provide minimally so that the child's welfare ends up as the state's concern, the state loses.

Is it justifiable to speak of the state as an entity with singular interests? In this case, there are two assumptions upon which this might be justified. The first is that the multitude of individual actors who make up the state have few contrary interests with respect to the depletion of state's resources. When parents—private parties—fail to provide for their children, state's resources are called upon. Since those resources are always scarce, legislators of all ideological persuasions would prefer to spend less rather than more of those resources so that they can fund equally or more worthy causes.[5] Thus, if states have any interest at all in children being reared adequately, legislators will always prefer—on the basis of their own self-interest—that this be done with private party resources. This is because all legislators have an interest in minimizing the tax burden on their constituents (in order to maximize their chances of reelection), and to maximize discretionary state resources to support their other goals. States need not constrain legislators to do their bidding in this instance, therefore. Legislators might be tempted to shift the burden of children's welfare to the state only if noncustodial fathers were a sufficiently powerful interest group to threaten reelection.

The second assumption refers to welfare states specifically. Welfare states are residual debtors in cases in which parents fail to provide adequately for their children. The debt accrues to the state apparatus as a whole, regardless of whether the individual actors making up that state believe that the claim is warranted, or not. This is embodied in the definition of a welfare state:

> A 'welfare state' is a state in which organized power is deliberately used (through policies and administration) in an effort to modify the play of market forces in at least three directions—first, by guaranteeing individuals and families a minimum income . . . second by narrowing the extent of insecurity by enabling individuals and families to meet 'social contingencies' (for example, sickness, old age and unemployment) which lead otherwise to individual and family crises; and third by ensuring that all citizens without distinction of status or class are offered the best standards available in relation to a certain agreed range of social services. (Briggs 1961, p. 228)

Therefore, I will use the notion of state interests when the state's resources are depleted by a failure of other parties to meet their obligations, or by a transfer of obligations from private parties to states. I will assume that in these instances, there are no significant internal state disputes.

There is another reason why states care about the welfare of children, and especially about the proper functioning of families. This is because states in heterogeneous societies depend upon their constituent groups to provide social order (Hechter, Friedman, and Kanazawa 1992). Social order is a by-product of the solidarity of those constituent groups. Therefore, when solidarity of the family decreases, so does the overall level of social order. Since the family historically has been such an important group for providing social control over the behavior of its members, particularly its young, the decline in family solidarity has important implications for the decline in social order (for example, the increase in drug use and crime rates among the young). States do provide direct social control to maintain social order, but it is far more costly to do so directly than to enjoy indirectly the by-products of the social control efforts of constituent groups.

One of the interesting issues that arises in the course of this study is why states have permitted the gradual erosion of the family if it is, in fact, so critical to states' own robustness.

The Historical Roots of the Structure of Indifference

At the heart of the structural changes that undermined the worth of the social bargain are the laws that made divorce relatively easy and that served as the foundation for the separation of obligations for children's well-being. Whereas the family had once been held accountable for nurture, education, and material support, and paternal right was borne out of those obligations, now mothers would become responsible for nurture, fathers for material support, and the state for education. How this occurred and how it shaped the working rules governing custody decisions are the subjects of this book.

Most child custody determinations favor mothers as sole physical custodians, even if legal custody is to be shared [see, for instance, Maccoby and Mnookin's (1992) study], and even if some states actively encouraged, as a matter of public policy, continuing primary roles for both parents. There is an institution—in Ostrom's sense of working rules—of maternal presumption: the notion that, under normal circumstances, separated and divorced mothers should be granted custody of their children. In the present time, questions about child custody are not posed from a standpoint of equal claim of mothers and fathers and are more often posed as if the child were already in the mother's embrace. Consequently, the framing of child custody decisions is such that the question at divorce becomes one of whether the child will remain under the mother's care and control or be taken from her wholly or in part.

This framing is in stark contrast to the institution governing custody prior to the late 1800s. During the nineteenth century and before, Roman, German, and Anglo-Saxon law placed children firmly in the embrace of their fathers, both during marriage and after it. The working rules reflected these laws, and there existed the presumption of paternal custody. The paternal custody presumption had greater legal support than maternal custody presumption does: women were often legal dependents themselves, and could not be awarded custody of their children, even after the death of the father, for the law had no means by which to award custody of one dependent to another.

Within the span of 40 years, roughly from 1880 to 1920, the presumption that divorced fathers should be granted custody of their children was changed everywhere. New laws were passed upholding the equal claims of mothers and fathers. These laws provided the basis for a new set of working rules governing custody, those favoring maternal custody. Judges issued decisions favoring mothers where they had previously favored fathers. The language of judicial decisions that had once called upon God, Nature, and Reason to undergird paternal custody awards now called upon God, Nature, and Reason to support maternal custody awards. An 1842 custody decision in the state of New Jersey held that

> We are informed by the first elementary books we read, that the authority of the father is superior to that of the mother. It is the doctrine of all civilized nations. It is according to the revealed law, the law of nature, and it prevails even with the wandering savage, who has received none of the lights of civilization.

In 1916, in the state of Washington, equally strong language appears to uphold an award of custody to a mother:

> Mother love is a dominant trait in even the weakest of women, and as a general thing surpasses the paternal affection for the common offspring, and, moreover, a child needs a mother's care even more than a father's. For these reasons courts are loathe to deprive the mother of the custody of her children, and will not do so unless it be shown clearly that she is so far an unfit and improper person to be intrusted with custody as to endanger the welfare of the children.[5]

A fundamental change had taken place in child custody awards in all Western countries that permitted divorce. This included Belgium, France, England, Germany, the Netherlands, Sweden, and Switzerland. The speed of the transition was quite variable, and the manner in which it came about reflected different political realities. Yet the beginning and the endpoint were the same everywhere: paternal custody had been the law and the norm; maternal custody became the norm.

Notes

1. Weiss and Willis (1985) utilized a collective goods analysis to model divorce settlements. Their model predicts the direction of custody rights and alimony transfers, and offers an explanation for why disparate spousal income increases the probability of divorce.

2. Hardin (1982) has an extensive discussion of public and collective goods. Pure public goods—which are difficult to identify empirically, are defined both by jointness of supply and impossibility of exclusion. Public and collective goods raise issues both about consumption and production. In the case of children, both are relevant. If parents (and others) can enjoy children without contributing

to their welfare (or without contributing their "fair share"), wherein lies the incentive for them to invest in their children?

3.   Furstenberg and Cherlin (1992, p. 95) observe that "Remarriage has complicated this system of exchange because it offers no clear-cut guidelines for assigning rights and obligations. Remarriage certainly expands the potential universe of kin, but does it also dilute the importance of each link? . . . this thinner form of kinship may not be an adequate substitute for the loss of relatives who had a stronger stake in the child's success. Through divorce and remarriage, individuals are related to more and more people, to each of whom they owe less and less."

4.   The following discussion of parent–child relation as a principal–agent one was prompted in part by a similar discussion of the physician–patient relation in Buchanan (1991).

5.   Freeland v. Freeland, 92 Wash. 482, 159 p. 698 (1916).

2

The Social Construction of the
Parent–Child Relation

A child has a biological mother and father but beyond that the connection among the three is socially constructed, and therefore is subject to negotiation and revision. This is true at the level of the individual family as well as at the broader societal level. The assignment of social meaning to familial relations is captured in the ritual of the ancient Romans in which the newborn child, not even yet washed of its mother's blood, is placed at its father's feet. If the father chose to raise it up, it signified his commitment to provide for it.[1] There is a similar ritual in modern Thailand (Rajhadhon 1965), in which the mother of the child lifts the basket in which the child is contained, calling out, "It is mine." There are other recurrent patterns, as well. A mother can leave her baby at a stranger's doorstep, or in a garbage dump; a father can leave mother and baby. These always were historical possibilities.

More subtle arrangements between parents and children that diverge from the ideal also are possible: exploitation of child labor, emotional, physical, and sexual abuse, and neglect all exist. These are the follies of parents. Children's consistent delinquency or mental illness also stress ideal parent–child relations. In actuality, the character of this relationship has an infinite range.

Societal proscriptions for parent–child relations are less varied and easier to characterize. Working rules governing custody—both legally and informally—are formulated in the context of the norms that constrain parent–child relations. Issues of child custody do not arise in all societies, however. If a child is to be raised by a community, or if the obligation for the child is encoded in clear genealogical rituals that begin with but ultimately go beyond biological parents, custody never arises as a social issue at all.

Consider, for instance, the Nairs of Malabar, where men and women have marriage-like liaisons, but men are never admitted to the matrilineal family group. Thus, a father has no control over his children, nor do they have claim over him or his property:

> The family, for all practical purposes, among the Nairs, consists of one's mother's mother and one's mother's mother's brother who is the male economic representative of the household, one's mother, mother's mother's brothers, mother's sisters, mother's sisters' children, and one's brothers and sisters. If any man were to be regarded as socially one's father, it would actually be the man who had been married and divorced from one's mother years before; for by Brahman law, a woman can enter into only one religious marriage. Here, then, is a family in which one biological parent has been socially eliminated. (Mead 1932, p. 37)

Divorce among the Nairs is irrelevant to the family standing and economic security of the child, and the issue of custody would never arise. Nor is it an issue among the Ibo of Nigeria:

> In Ibo society there can be no question of the custody of the children when a marriage is dissolved. They belong to the husband's family. It was largely for them that the marriage was contracted and the bride-price paid in the first place. The question may be raised as to how they can be taken care of without their mother, but the truth is that the mother's care is not necessary. (Davis 1944, p. 702)

When kinship is an important principle of social organization, the society need not be a primitive one to find an answer to the question of custody of the children following divorce. In China

> The immediate family was subordinate in nearly every respect to the extended family . . . The young bride was subordinate to the older females in her husband's extended household, and the husband was subordinate to his grandfather, father, or older brother. The household was frequently quite large, so that the children were surrounded by adults other than their mother and father . . . [upon divorce] the child necessarily remained in the father's household, where he continued to find the milieu much as it had been before. (Davis 1944, pp. 703–704)

When the child is firmly ensconced in a familial structure in which divorce has no implications for its security, custody is irrelevant. This suggests two questions. One is how and why it is that our own society has followed a path that, at least from the child's point of view, offers a far less reliable source of continuing welfare than ones in which children are embedded in an inviolate relationship of obligation. A second question has to do with the nature of custody arrangements: how and why these?

Marriage as the Basis of Family Structure

In matrilineal and patrilineal systems, the fundamental tension between family groups—and marriage partners—is an assumption upon which the security of the children is predicated. There is no need for the father's kin and the mother's kin to find harmony for the child's future to be assured. There is no need for the father and mother to find love and continued attachment for the child's future to be assured. The child's future will be as bright or as bleak as the lineal future is.

In bilateral systems, the child's future depends largely upon the marriage relation. Modern marriage is a dyadic relation. Structurally it is tenuous, for as Simmel (1950) explained, a group of two depends upon both for its life, but only one for its death. From the child's point of view, the family disappears when the marriage dissolves. Though the child is a member of the group, he or she has no say in whether it persists, and since the family structure rests entirely on marriage, it matters little whether there is one child in the family or four. As Mead (1932, p. 26) recognized:

> Although the recognition of the marriage bond as the basis of family relationship is the closest approximation to biological facts of mating and parenthood, and is found among many of the simplest peoples, it actually *represents a weak family organization when the family is viewed as the economic and social kinship structure which rears and gives status to children*; for the biological family, with its pallid recognition of two sets of antagonistic kinship allegiances—to the mother's kin and to the father's kin—is a status-giving group founded upon a relationship which lacks the permanency of that of a blood group. The biological family can be shattered by divorce or death and the child left in an indeterminate position, economically, socially, and affectionally, which is impossible in any society which stresses blood ties at the expense of the marriage tie. (Emphasis added)

Issues of custody arise, then, only in certain family structures. Variations in children's security following divorce do not emanate principally from their parents' allegiance to them, but rather from the structure of family social organization. Families forged by marriage produce the highest level of insecurity for children, for the family itself dissolves when the marriage bond is broken by divorce. Formal and informal rules governing custody are constrained by these family structures.

Providing security for children is most challenging in a nuclear bilateral family system. When there is a high degree of dependence of the husband and wife on the marriage, so high that it nearly precludes divorce, the child's security is a by-product. As argued in Chapter 1, however, the dependence of adults on marriage has declined over time.

Another indirect source of security might come from the presence of extended family members, a kind of informal kinship structure. There is nothing, however, to compel relatives to make continuing contributions to the welfare of their extended family's children, so this too is an unreliable source of security for those children. These ties have grown weaker over time, as primordial social relations have given way to modern forms of social organization.

The most explicit way to address the issue of security for children in this kind of family form is to specify parental obligations to children and to prevent the dissolution of the family, to disallow divorce. Until a century ago, this was the dominant solution. Custody laws were formulated initially in a system in which divorce was granted only in exceptional circumstances, and in which death was the more common form of familial disruption.

Thus, in a family system resting on marriage, ensuring children's security is problematic in marriage but even more so following divorce. As the frequency of divorce increased, these issues became more pressing: Just how were children to be provided for when their future was made uncertain by the divorce of their parents?

The Logic of Custody Laws: Blackstone on Parent–Child Relations

To understand the logic of child custody institutions following divorce—both presently and historically—it is first necessary to understand the original ideal-type conception of parent–child relations in marriage-based bilateral family systems. For this purpose, Blackstone's *Commentaries* (1765) is unequalled. It is an essay on constitutional law— constitutional here meaning legal and fundamental, the constituted system—and is considered "the most important legal treatise ever written in the English language. It was the predominant lawbook in England and America in the century after its publication and played a unique role in the development of the fledgling American legal system" (Katz 1979, p. iii).

For Blackstone, parent–child relations were one of four private relations (three "natural" and one supplementary) requiring legal regulation:

> The three great relations in private life are, 1. That of *master and servant*; which is founded in convenience, whereby a man is directed to call in the assistance of others, where his own skill and labor will not be sufficient to answer the cares incumbent upon him. 2. That of *husband and wife*; which is founded in nature, but modified by civil society: the one directing man to

continue and multiply his species, the other prescribing the manner in which that natural impulse must be confined and regulated. 3. That of *parent and child*, which is consequential to that of marriage, being it's principal end and design: and it is by virtue of this relation that infants are protected, maintained, and educated. But since the parents, on whom this care is primarily incumbent, may be snatched away by death or otherwise, before they have completed their duty, the law has therefore provided a fourth relation; 4. That of *guardian and ward*, which is a kind of artificial parentage, in order to supply the deficiency, whenever it happens, of the natural. (Blackstone [1765] 1979, p. 410)

The grouping of these four is not accidental: these are all conceived of as hierarchical relations, in which the law regulates the behavior of the more powerful toward the less powerful. The law might have focused on the obligations of the servant toward the master, the wife toward the husband, and the child toward the parent. Instead, regulation is founded in the *obligations of those who are bound to others* either naturally or through status position. It specifies the conditions of their dominance and then constrains their behavior.

What, then, are the obligations of the parent to the child? The parent's responsibilities "principally consist in three particulars; their maintenance, their protection, and their education" (434). These were considerable; first of all, maintenance:

The duty of parents to provide for the *maintenance* of their children is a principle of natural law; an obligation . . . laid on them not only by nature herself, but by their own proper act, in bringing them into the world: for they would be in the highest manner injurious to their issue, if they only gave the children life, that they might afterwards see them perish . . . And thus the children will have a perfect *right* of receiving maintenance from their parents. (435)

Though maintenance of children might be a natural law, states were wise to enforce the duty. At the same time, Blackstone expressed a familiar wish that it need not be so:

The municipal laws of all well-regulated states have taken care to enforce this duty: though providence has done it more effectually than any laws, by implanting in the breast of every parent that natural . . . or insuperable degree of affection, which not even the deformity of person or mind, not even the wickedness, ingratitude, and rebellion of children, can totally suppress or extinguish. (435)

The duty to protect one's children needed the law's constraint rather than its positive sanction: "protection; which is also a natural duty, but rather permitted than enjoined by in municipal laws: nature, in this respect, working so strongly as to need rather a check than a spur" (438).

The third obligation, that of providing education, was not inconsiderable. The parent's duty was to educate according to the parents' station in life. Blackstone seemed to think the argument an obvious one:

> It is not easy to imagine or allow, that a parent has conferred any considerable benefit upon his child, by bringing him into the world; if he afterwards entirely neglects his culture and education, and suffers him to grow up like a mere beast, to lead a life useless to others, and shameful to himself. (439)

These three obligations formed the basis of domination of the parent over the child. The dominant relation between the two did not derive from any primal right. Blackstone made this explicit: "The *power* of parents over their children is derived from the former consideration, their duty; this authority being given them, partly to enable the parent more effectually to perform his duty, and partly as a recompense for his care and trouble in the faithful discharge of it" (440). Power was purposeful, not a right deriving from natural domination.

This was principally the father's power. Why so? It was because the three cornerstones of the parent–child relation—maintenance, protection, and education—were, given the extant social structure, the father's duties. Much has subsequently been made of the father's right to his child's estate and labor, and even more about the mother's lack of access to her child's estate and labor, but these are but a minor part of the relationship. The oft-quoted phrase, "a mother, as such, is entitled to no power, but only to reverence and respect" (441), has been irresponsibly severed from its context. Indeed, this phrase is embedded in a section discussing the father's responsibility to protect his children from "too early and precipitate marriages," and immediately following this dictum, Blackstone wrote:

> A father has no other power over his sons estate, than as his trustee or guardian; for, though he may receive the profits during the child's minority, yet he must account for them when he comes of age. He may indeed have the benefit of his children's labour while they live with him, and are maintained by him: but this is no more than he is entitled to from his apprentices or servants. The legal power of a father (for a mother, as such, is entitled to no power, but only to reverence and respect) the power of a father, I say, over the persons of his children ceases at the age of twenty-one. (441)

Power is neither absolute nor unconstrained; it rests upon obligation. When the obligation ceases, so does the power. And for those with no obligations—mothers—there is no power.

These are hierarchical relations, specifying the conditions of dominance, hence the distinction between legitimate and illegitimate children that is so difficult to understand from our modern vantage point. Illegitimate children exist outside relations of hierarchy, those very relations that led to the legal specification of obligation. Children produced out of wedlock are conceived by individuals with no status in the law. Sexual relations between the unmarried were sexual relations among legal equals (the only relevant status being as consenting adults). Sexual relations between husbands and wives were among unequals, and therefore regulated by law.

This logic extended to second husbands (of widows). By marrying, he assumed the obligation of the husband toward the wife, which included the assumption of her debts. Thus, he was obligated to provide maintenance for the children of her first husband until *her* death. The second husband did not become the father of the children, but he nonetheless had responsibility for those children, responsibility that derived from marriage.

When the father was absent—usually owing to his death—he was expected, by right and responsibility to appoint a guardian. The guardian was both the tutor, in charge of maintenance and education of the child, and the curator, in charge of the estate of the child. The relation between the guardian and ward was explicitly intended to be the same as that between the father and child (Blackstone 1765, p. 450).

Blackstone did not consider the problem of custody following divorce. Yet when others would come to do so, they would naturally turn to the logic governing the parent–child relation within marriage. Since this relation was defined almost exclusively in terms of the father's obligations toward the child, it followed that the father would be called upon to continue to honor those obligations. Hence the expectation of paternal custody.

Paternal Presumption in Child Custody following Divorce

As divorce became more frequent—although the change in the rate was very slow in the beginning—child custody decisions were more often brought into the court's arena. Yet fully articulated child custody law was unavailable.[2] Thus, when judges were called upon to find relevant law upon which to base their decisions, they turned to the laws that defined the parent–child relation in marriage.

In both England and the United States judges relied heavily on English case law in defending their decisions. Most child custody decisions favored fathers in their superior claim to custody. Partiality to the father rested on his obligations toward the child. Thus a Rhode Island custody decision in 1824 held that the father's right to custody "is not on account of any absolute right of the father, but for the benefit of the infant, the law presuming it be under the nurture and care of his natural protector, both for maintenance and education.[3] Similar language can be found in court decisions in other states, as well. In an 1860 New Hampshire decision, the judge wrote, "It is a well-settled doctrine of the common law, that the father is entitled to the custody of his minor children, as against the mother and everybody else; that he is bound for their maintenance and nurture, and has the corresponding right to their obedience and their services."[4] In Virginia in 1878, a decision finding in favor of a father explained, "the father is the legal custodian of the minor children, and they will not be taken from his custody without the strongest reasons therefore."[5]

There was, however, in the United States an additional supposition regarding paternal superiority in custody: fathers were considered superior *guardians* of their children:

> The fundamental idea upon which the entire legal conception of such guardianship rests is, that it is a mere agency or instrumentality of government for the purpose of according to infants the protection of its laws. In true legal conception, a guardian is simply the agent or trustee of the government. His authority is that delegated by the government; his powers and functions are limited and defined by the nature and purpose of the authority thus delegated; and in and for their exercise he is entirely subject and accountable to it. The legal status of a guardian is purely that of a trustee—his trust differing from other trusts only in this respect, that it is "of all trusts the most sacred." (Hochheimer 1891, p. 4)

Unlike in England, where guardianship covered only heirs-apparent, the American version extended to all children. The natural guardianship of parents served both the interests of the child and of the public.[6] As such, parents were not free to divest themselves of the guardianship of their children.[7] Nonetheless, guardianship awards were benefits of trust that a government placed in an individual to satisfy the interests of the child.

It was never as clear in the United States as in England that fathers held the *right* of custody. Whereas *habeas corpus* was used frequently by fathers to recover possession of their children when they had been denied them by mothers or third parties, this procedure was granted much less recognition in the United States.

In both England and the United States, it was clear, however, that fathers were preferred in custody, and though the criterion upholding that preference might have differed in some regards, it led to the same consequences: fathers were granted custody of their children more often than were mothers.

Preference for fathers in custody was not a peculiarity of Anglo-American law. In France, where relations between parents and children were circumscribed by Roman law in the South and Germanic customary law in the North, paternal power held sway, tied to extensive obligations. There may have been a difference in emphasis, in that *paterfamilias* recognized the husband's monopoly over the means of social control within individual families, but this recognition was paired with a monopoly over responsibility and obligation, as well. The Germanic counterpart also included rights, power, and responsibility in the person of the father, but with one difference: his family was one among several equal families, each with its own patriarch, making up a larger kinship group. The results were both a check on unbridled power as well as a widening sphere of obligation, especially toward children: this conception of the family (*mundium*) could be interpreted as "an operational legal concept embedded in custom and administered by the kinship group, [which] functioned as a *guideline* to protect children" (Blakesley 1981, p. 290).

The extensive enunciation of the father's responsibilities and obligations to his children was deeply embedded in the institution of the family and the legal doctrine that governed family relations. As long as the social organization of families remained relatively unchanged, there would seem to be little that could shake the father's status with respect to his children. Yet the social organization of families was changed fundamentally by the increasing access of husbands and wives to divorce. Divorce posed at first challenges to the preference for fathers over mothers (and others), and, ultimately, a change in the preference altogether.

Challenges to Paternal Preference in England and the United States

In England

In England in the 1800s, three cases in particular captured the attention of the newspaper-reading public. Later, in 1839, they would provide grit for those who would speak on behalf of a new law before the House of Lords. *Rex v. De Manneville* (1804)[8] was perhaps the most graphic: an eight-month-old baby was taken, literally, from his mother's breast. The mother sought redress in both the Court of King's Bench and later in the Chancery. In both settings, she utilized the venue to continue to breast-feed the baby, although she ultimately lost in both courts.

Public outcry peaked around the case of *Rex v. Greenhill* (1836).[9] Because Mrs. Greenhill refused the Court of King's Bencorder to give over her three daughters, all under six, to their father, who was known for his boundless cruelty, she was imprisoned for contempt of court (Graveson and Crane 1957). The victorious counsel for Mr. Greenhill happened to be Mr. Serjeant Talfourd.

Talfourd, feeling his conscience compromised by the case, and no doubt having been subject to the slings and arrows of the public outcry, introduced several bills designed to change the status quo. The first, in 1838, made provision for a mother's access to her children, though not custody of them. This was opposed on the grounds that it might allow for an immoral mother's influence on her children. Thus, the next bill suggested that judges in Equity might be permitted to award mothers custody of children under seven and access to older children provided that they had not been proved to be adulterous. This prompted his now-famous, though largely irrelevant remark that when the court would find in favor of the mother it would be "simply putting the mother of legitimate children in the same situation as a mother of bastard children" since mothers of illegitimate children had custody of them by default.

This second bill prompted an avalanche of protest on the grounds that it would undermine the stability of marriage. It might encourage disputes to arise between husbands and wives and would provide no deterrent to a woman who wished to leave her marriage. Those who favored this bill made their arguments on the grounds of injustice to mothers. Those who opposed it argued that nothing would constrain a woman outside of marriage to do her duty to her children, and, further, that children could not be served by spending seven years or less with one parent, only then to be transferred to the other.

The Infants Custody Act of 1839 (also known as Talfourd's Act) passed and served to expand the discretionary power of the Court of Chancery to control the custody of a child under seven years of age, should the mother make application for such consideration.

Further acts were passed in 1857 and 1886, both expanding the courts' discretionary powers. The Matrimonial Causes Act of 1857 granted the Divorce Court discretionary powers in the matters of custody of children. Additionally, the Court of Chancery was free to allow maternal custody until the age of 16, instead of 7. Further, mothers who had been adulterous wives were no longer forbidden to petition for access and custody. Finally, parents could make deeds of separation with custody provisions, though these were not to be considered binding.[10]

The most far-reaching of the bills was the 1886 Custody of Infants Bill. On the surface it seemed to be motivated by a desire to remedy the powerlessness of mothers following the death of fathers, and, indeed, one if its provisions was that a mother would assume guardianship of her children following the death of the father if the father had appointed no guardian, and would assume joint guardianship if he had. In addition, mothers were to be allowed to appoint guardians following their own deaths, provided that the father had already died.

With respect to custody following divorce, however, the provisions were extensive. First, all restrictions on the right of appeal for custody and access were removed: a mother of any moral character or blame was permitted to make a case before the Court of Chancery for a child of any age or condition. Second, and most striking, courts were granted the jurisdiction, *without any constraint*, to grant custody as they saw fit. Without any constraint meant that the common law rights of the father were no longer paramount. Third, blame in the case of divorce was relegated to a secondary role with respect to custody.

Other acts followed, including the 1925 Guardianship of Infants Act, explicitly upholding the principle of the equal rights of parents to the guardianship of their children. Finally, to close the circle, the Administration of Justice Act of 1928 granted *fathers* the right to apply for the custody of their legitimate children.

In the United States

Challenges to and changes in paternal preference in custody of children in the United States were undertaken both at the state and federal levels in response to or in concert with changes in divorce. The years in which this occurred in different states are given in Table 2.1. In 20 states, no preference between parents was given. In six states, there was a specific provision to override the common-law rule of paternal preference. Five states codified the equality-through-culpability rule, stating that the innocent party in the divorce is to be preferred. Eleven states implied mother-preference, but in six of these it was expressed through her greater claim to maintenance for the children. Only three states implied father-preference.

What these statutes all have in common is strong language establishing the court's power as entirely discretionary in the matter of child custody. There were consistent attempts to specify the manner in which

Table 2.1.   Year of Legislative Recognition of Equal Parental Rights in Custody, by State

State	Year	State	Year
Alabama	1923	Mississippi	1930
Alaska	1931	Missouri	1929
Arizona	1928	Montana	1921
Arkansas	1921	Nebraska	1929
California	1933	Nevada	1929
Colorado	1921	New Hampshire	1926
Connecticut	1930	New Jersey	1910
Delaware	1927	New Mexico	1929
D.C.	1929	New York	1930
Florida	1921	North Carolina	1927
Georgia	1926[a]	North Dakota	1913
Hawaii	1925[a]	Ohio	1931
Idaho	1919	Oregon	1930
Illinois	1931	Pennsylvania	1920
Indiana	1926	Rhode Island	1923
Iowa	1927	South Carolina	1922
Kansas	1923[b]	South Dakota	1929
Kentucky	1922	Tennessee	1932
Louisiana	1915[c]	Texas	1928[a]
Maine	1930	Utah	1933
Maryland	1929	Vermont	1921
Massachusetts	1932	Virginia	1930
Minnesota	1923	Washington	1922

[a]Father's common law preference was preserved to some degree.
[b]Kansas guaranteed parental equality through constitutional provision.
[c]In a case of decision between father and mother, the father's authority is to prevail.

discretion ought to be exercised in custody awards. Five states suggest that judges should take account of the age and sex of the child. Two states suggest that judges should consult children as to their preferences, if they are of sufficient age. Twelve states mention the safety and well-being of children as worthy of consideration, and most mention the child's happiness, comfort, and spiritual welfare as being germane. Four states suggested that the character of the parents was relevant in custody determinations. In all states, without exception, the court's discretion was absolute.

At the federal level, in every year from 1897 to 1923 there was an attempt in Congress to pass a Uniform Marriage and Divorce Act, which sought to bring marriage and divorce law under federal jurisdiction. Had it been successful, it would have served as a guide to custody, as well. But the substance of the debates—which will be taken up in Chapter 4—suggested that it would have been no different from state laws, and also would have given absolute discretion in matters of custody to courts.

Consequences for the Security of Children

In England and the United States, the new legislation replaced a relatively certain, if sometimes unjust, set of laws governing custody with ones that were strikingly uncertain because they rested with the determination of a single individual, the judge, acting on behalf of a monolithic but changing and unknowable entity, the state. The removal of the long-held guidelines that favored fathers gave rise to the troubling question of just what rules judges would use, other than relying on their own predilections, in awarding custody.

Paternal rights within intact families had been a system with a considerable degree of logic. The inequality of the parent–child relation was explicit, thereby allowing for the specification of the father's (the agent's) obligations toward the child. That the obligations were the father's alone from a theoretical point of view privatized the child; responsibility for the child's welfare could not be shifted to another party. Without divorce, the child could depend upon the family to continue in its risk-reducing capacity during childhood.

Most of the structural advantages offered by the system of paternal right and preference for paternal custody disappeared with the changes in custody law. When paternal preference gave way to roughly equal preference between mothers and fathers in custody, little consideration was given to the obligations that were the rationale for the preference for fathers. Equality of parents before the court in applications for custody were not accompanied by equality of parental obligations toward the child. Indeed, when paternal preference was supplanted, the notion of obligation vanished. In its place came vague directives about the best interests of the child.

The confusion that resulted was considerable, particularly with respect to the obligation to provide for children. Men were better able to provide for children than were women, but what was the logic by which the courts could compel them to do so? Previously, obligation had been tied to paternal right, as in England, or paternal preference, as in the United States. Fathers could be preferred in custody on account of their superior financial position. But what reason could be given to compel them to pay when they were not the preferred custodial party?

Interestingly, the first step toward severing the link between preference and the obligation to pay came in the reduction—to the absolute minimum—of the amount to be paid. A slew of case law upheld the *minimum* liability of the parent for that which was deemed essential.[11]

From these cases came a set of principles of support: fathers would not have to purchase anything but necessities; fathers would be liable only for what was to be required to relieve children from absolute want; if a child left the father, the father would be responsible for his upkeep, but each article's need would have to be strictly proven. These principles led to the conclusion that "The father is liable only for a bare maintenance of his infant children, who have not property of their own, where they are taken from his custody after a divorce and transferred to the custody of his mother" (Field 1888, p. 61). The contrast between this and the imperatives of Blackstone is striking. The better part of a century would be spent trying to redefine paternal financial obligation; these matters still are far from resolved (Mnookin and Weisberg, 1982).

A new source of uncertainty was introduced, as well: judges' discretion. Whereas there were, in some cases, weak directives with regard to children's welfare, there were no directives with regard to obligations. Basing decisions on children's welfare rather than on parents' obligations had several flaws. First, just what constituted children's well-being was murky. Should the judge's estimation of a child's happiness with one parent as against another be the guiding criterion? Or should the judge's estimation of the child's material well-being take precedence? How should the child's present needs be balanced against the child's future needs? The focus on children's welfare served only to expand discretion. Yet the argument that children's well-being ought to be the court's principal consideration turned out to be so enormously compelling symbolically and rhetorically that questions about what constitutes the child's best interest are still of abiding concern.

There was another problem with the uncertainty inherent in the expansion of judicial discretion. What sorts of implications would this have for the incentive structure for parents' contributions to their children? These implications would depend upon the perception of how judges would come to define children's well-being. If nurture or mothering was to be given primary importance, what incentive would fathers have for maximum contributions to their children's material welfare? If, on the other hand, material welfare or education were to be the guiding principle, what incentive would mothers have for maximum contributions to their children's emotional well-being? The specialization of mothers and fathers that might be assumed or demonstrated to contribute to an optimal division of labor in intact families would lead only to a zero-sum competition in divorced ones.

Equality of parents in applications for custody was borne out of increased judicial discretion rather than clarity about children's welfare. In England and in most states in the United States, there was no answer in the new laws to the question of which parent was to be the preferred custodian.

Despite the rhetoric of children's welfare, it was not clear that there were any clear gains for children. In addition to the disadvantages inherent in divorced families for children came the severing of parental right and obligation. The obligation to provide, to educate, and to protect were measurable and enforceable, at least conceivably. Whereas parents might fight vehemently for the custody of their children and use arguments predicated on their children's presumed welfare, parents would not be asked to demonstrate their relative suitability in providing for the full range of their children's needs over the period of their childhood.

The fundamental question guiding custody was thus changed from "Who has the obligation for this child?" to "Who has the greater claim to this child?"

Notes

1. The image of the father in a *paterfamilias* system deciding about the fate of his child is a powerful and recurrent one. It has been parlayed often into an image of male domination, but I suspect that J. M. Barrie captured the sentiment much more closely in *Peter Pan* (1911, pp. 3–4): "For a week or two after Wendy came it was doubtful whether they would be able to keep her, as she was another mouth to feed. Mr. Darling was frightfully proud of her, but he was very honourable, and he sat on the edge of Mrs. Darling's bed, holding her hand, and calculating expenses, while she looked at him imploringly. She wanted to risk it, come what might, but that was not his way; his way was with a pencil and a piece of paper . . . at last Wendy just got through."

2. For a discussion of the development of custody law from 1790 to the late 1800s in the United States, see Mason (1994).

3. *U. S. v. Green*, 3 Mason 482, 26 Fed. Cases 15, 256 (Cir. Ct. R. I. 1824).

4. *State v. Richardson*, 40 NH, 272 (1860).

5. *Latham v. Latham*, 30 Grat 307 (1878).

6. *U.S. v. Green*, 3 Mason 482, 26 Fed. Cases 15, 256 (Cir. Ct. R. I. 1824); *Giles v. Giles* 30 Neb. 624, 46 N.W. 916 (1890); *State ex rel. Filbert v. Schroeder*, 37 Neb. 571, 56 N.W. 307 (1893); *Nugent v. Powell*, 4 Wyom. 173, 33 P. 23 (1893).

7. *Torrington v. Norwich*, 21 Conn. 543 (1852); *State ex rel. Mayne v. Baldwin*, 5 N.J. Eq. 454 (1846); *Albert v Perry*, 14 N.J. Eq. 540 (1862); *State ex rel. Hodgdon v. Libbey*, 44 N.H. 321 (1862); *Washaw v. Gimble*, 50 Ark. 351, 7 S. W. 389 (1888); In re Lewis, 88 N.C. 31 (1883); In re Scarritt, 76 Mo. 565 (1882).

8. *Rex v. De Manneville*, 5 East 221 (1804).

9. *Rex v. Greenhill*, 4 A. & E. 624 (1836).

10. The 1879 case of *Besant v. Besant* tested the robustness of these agreements. Mrs. Besant was an atheist, and even though the Reverend Besant agreed that she should have custody of their daughter, the court intervened and returned custody to her father.

11. *Hunt v. Thompson*, 3 Scam. 179, 36 Am. Dec. 538 (Ill. 1841); *Varney v. Young*, 11 Vt. 258 (1839); *Raymond v. Loyl*, 10 Barb. 483 (N.Y. 1851); *Stanton v. Wilson*, 3 Day 37 (Conn. 1808); *Van Valkinburgh v. Watson & Watson*, 13 Johns. 480 (N.Y. 1816); *Townsend v. Burnham*, 33 N. H. 270 (1856); *Pidgin v. Cram*, 8 N.H. 350 (1836); *Owen v. White*, 5 Port. 435 (Ala. 1837).

3

Received Explanations for the Change to Maternal Preference in Child Custody

The greater claim of fathers to their children was predicated on their obligations. That they were better able to meet those obligations than mothers certainly emanated from their more powerful positions outside the family. Yet the judicial discretion embodied in changes in custody laws that paved the way for maternal preference in custody occurred prior to social changes that significantly altered the position of women in society. Mothers were generally no better able to meet parental obligations to children than they had been prior to the change in laws. How, then, did mothers come to be the preferred custodians of children?

The single most commonly held view avers that there was, in the nineteenth century, a growing emphasis on motherhood that was inextricably linked to a changing view of childhood (Zainaldin 1979; Vandepol 1982; Grossberg 1983, 1985; Boris and Bardaglio 1983; Atkins and Hoggett 1984; Boyd 1989). Changes in custody reflected the increasing sensitivity of judges to a growing cultural emphasis on childhood, female domesticity, and distinctive sex roles. These had their roots in the social changes of family life in the West (Ariès 1962; Stone 1979; Shorter 1975) in which the family had become conjugal, nuclear, highly differentiated and specialized, private, and child-centered. The household had changed from a unit of production to one of consumption. Men were going further from the home for employment, so that the management of the family increasingly devolved upon the mother. This differentiation in sexual roles drew reinforcement from the antebellum cultural ideal of "true womanhood," according to which a woman's purity and innocence suited her for the duties of childrearing and home management. Domesticity became the ideal of womanhood, and the home her exclusive domain, leading to a redistribution of authority in the household, with the wife becoming the equal of the husband. These social changes affected legislators and judges as they struggled with family law, and they began to include a consideration of the welfare of the child and of parental qualifications. Gender roles, parental conduct, the image of childhood, and the age of the child became important components in custody decisions. There was a new faith in developmental notions of childhood, in a nurture-based definition of child welfare, and in women's innate abilities for childrearing (Grossberg 1985).

The Differentiation of Roles and the Emphasis on Motherhood

The argument that children need their mothers seems self-evident from a modern perspective. Clearly this was not always seen to be the case. Modern motherhood was socially and culturally defined (Bloch 1978), and it was this new conception, some argue, that explains the shift in preference from fathers to mothers in custody.

Bloch (1978) traces this development from the late eighteenth century. Using literature pertaining to mothering that circulated in America (although much of it originated in England) between the late seventeenth and early nineteenth centuries, she suggests that the change in the definition of motherhood arose as a result of three factors: the disappearance of servants and other nonkin from the home, the removal of men's work and production from the home, and the increasing depiction of women as morally superior to men.

Prior to the late eighteenth century, the ideal images of women appearing in the literature did not focus on women's role as a parent but rather on women as Christians and wives. There was little attention to women as mothers, and to the extent that mothering did draw literary attention, it was childbearing and breast-feeding that were discussed. There was little written emphasis on emotional bonds.

The literature on childrearing gave fathers as much or more notice and appreciation as mothers. In writings about childhood education following nursing, there was an assumption that parenting was something largely taken care of by fathers, or parenting was defined without reference to gender (Bloch 1978; Margolis 1984). In general, then, motherhood was devalued relative to fatherhood. Cultural assumptions about the inferiority of women as less rational and more emotional made them inappropriate to the task of childrearing that was to emphasize self-discipline and theological understanding. Moreover, mothers typically engaged in other tasks besides childrearing, taking care of basic household tasks and helping husbands with their crafts, trades, and enterprises.

In the late eighteenth century, Bloch (1978) notes a new conception of motherhood that appeared in the literature. Fathers began to recede into the background in discussions of the domestic education of children, and there was a growing emphasis on the importance of proper maternal care during infancy. These changes in definition reflected broader social changes, first evident in England, but also underway in the United States. Most important was the removal of fathers' places of work from the home. Fathers had less contact with their children, childrearing responsibilities became less diffuse, and mothers played a more exclusive role than they had in the past.

Not only were women increasingly responsible by themselves for childrearing, they also became more exclusively preoccupied with their maternal roles. Women were less able to assist their husbands, leading to a withering of their traditional economic roles and they were, at the same time, left as primary caretakers of their children. The new emphasis on the mother–child dyad would have been inconceivable a hundred years earlier because the conditions whereby women could devote themselves exclusively to their children did not exist (Margolis 1984).

What was the purpose of the exaltation of motherhood? One answer was that the emphasis on maternity helped to solve the so-called "woman question" (Margolis 1984). Once women's productive skills were no longer needed, motherhood was the answer to the question of how to occupy their time. The care of young children came to be viewed as a full-time task, requiring special knowledge, ultimately important to the well-being of the nation. Outside employment was not considered an option; advice givers argued that paid employment was incompatible with mothering and homemaking. Middle class women were to devote themselves to producing high quality children who would take their place in business and industry (Ryan 1981). By 1860, there were clearly separated spheres (Ryan 1981).

The Connection between Motherhood and Childhood Socialization

Changing views of childhood were concurrent with the new emphasis on motherhood. In the colonial period, there was little sense that children were a unique group: childhood was short and children worked at a young age (Margolis 1984). But in the period from 1785 to 1820, ideologies regarding children began to change. By 1800, Calvinist views of infant damnation had given way to the Lockean doctrine of *tabula rasa*. In the middle class, children began to be seen as individuals with a special need for nurturing rather than as miniature adults whose natural inclinations toward evil had to be broken. This new thinking placed a bigger burden on parents since failure in childrearing could no longer be blamed on native corruption. The *tabula rasa* idea gave way to the notion of children as beings of great purity and innocence. Mothers alone had the power to transform malleable infants into moral, productive adults.

Parenting had to prepare children for a new kind of adult life since the child's future was no longer determined by the father through inheritance, apprenticeship, and the like (Matthaei 1982). Among the well-to-do, sons' futures depended on their success in the labor market and daughters' futures on their success in the marriage market. Thus, parenting a son meant teaching him to be a self-seeking competitive individual and parenting a daughter meant preparing her to be a mother and a help-meet for one of these new individuals. Thus, during the nineteenth century, the conception of childhood as a distinct life stage emerged, first among the middle and upper classes. Parenting no longer meant putting the child to work, but rather developing the skills necessary to act responsibly in society.

Why did women come to be responsible for this task? It might appear that it was more appropriately the man's task. But since men were now actively involved in competition and self-advancement, they could not be expected to nurture individuality in others, the new task of parenting.

Thus, in England and the United States, the nineteenth century culture of domesticity—the sharp dichotomy between the home and the economic world that paralleled the contrast between male and female natures, the designation of the home as women's sole and proper sphere, the moral superiority of women, and the idealization of the women's function as a mother—was superimposed on the older European traditions that proclaimed the inferiority of women (Harris 1978).

Who Benefited from the Emphasis on Motherhood?

It is tempting to conclude that children were the primary beneficiaries of the increasing emphasis on motherhood. Yet if that is the case, the benefit to children was an unintended consequence.

One possibility is that business elites might have had further interests in emphasizing the domestic sphere of women (Margolis 1984). The lower wages of women could be justified by the notion that women's work was temporary or supplemental. Further, men could be encouraged to work harder and longer to avoid the stigma of having working wives.

Another possibility is that children were increasingly coming to be seen as national resources. Badinter's (1981) discussion of France and

Davin's (1978) discussion of England address this issue. They argue that the modern, sacrificing, loving mother arose in response to the desire to increase the population. High infant mortality rates were contradictory to this aim, and to the extent that infant mortality owed to maternal practices (wet nursing, in particular), women's behaviors would have to be changed (Badinter 1981). As a result women were promised prestige, the love of their husbands and children, and the opportunity to make an impact on society, if they turned to their maternal duties. Middle class women—who had fewer alternatives than either their richer or poorer counterparts—were the first to respond.

How would they be exhorted to turn to these duties? One argument, directed at men as well as women, was that human beings were important for the state both for wealth and military power. Davin (1978) argues that in the British case, the appreciation of the importance of children was encouraged by economic and political competition from Germany and the United States, as well as Japan.

Another argument was that women should not resist nature. After all, nature had created women so that they could feed their young. If they did resist, nature would take its revenge with disease, husbands would be fickle, and God would take note. Yet another argument was that maternal love was an integral part of the road to familial happiness: families would begin with the love between a husband and wife that would find form in offspring, parents would love their children as a result, and women would turn enthusiastically to their care and nurture.

However compelling, or weak, these arguments might have been, motherhood came to be viewed as a powerful vehicle through which women yielded broad social influence. Middle class women might have hesitated (Badinter 1981), but it was not merely a matter of choice: structural constraints would keep middle class women firmly in place.

Consequences for Custody Decisions

What resulted, according to some scholars, was a growing attempt to balance husbands' and wives' rights, and to give greater consideration to children's rights. The application of the new conceptions of psychological, cultural, and social principles was evident in courts' decisions. For instance, the conception of female domesticity led to a sense that mothers' claims ought to be paid some attention. Beliefs about child development suggested that young children required the ministry of their mothers. These strains are to be seen in three dominant explanations of the change in preference for mothers in custody over fathers. One is a law review article written by Jamil Zainaldin in 1979, another is a chapter in Michael Grossberg's book *Governing the Hearth* (1985), and the last is Susan Maidment's study, *Child Custody and Divorce* (1984). Due to the scarcity of research on this topic, each of these texts has greatly influenced the terms in which change in custody has come to be understood.

Received Knowledge on the Subject of the Change in Child Custody Laws

Zainaldin's Argument

Zainaldin (1979) comes to the question of custody through his consideration of adoption. His inquiry begins with an historical fact: the passage of an 1851 adoption law in Massachusetts that was radical in its departure from English law, legislation, and precedent. English domestic law consistently had prohibited the transfer of parental rights to third parties, and had never given primacy to the interests of the adoptees. The new Massachusetts law explicitly took into account both the welfare of the child and the qualifications of the proposed parents. One would think that such a striking departure from past practice would be widely remarked upon, yet this happened with hardly any public notice or legislative debate, and no notice from newspapers. Zainaldin remarks, "There is, then, no clear explanation for why the legislature passed the law when it did" (1043). The very same conclusion could be made about the changes in child custody law.

The impetus for the change in the adoption statute came, according to Zainaldin, from the diffuse new understanding of childhood and family that had permeated society by the nineteenth century, no more so than in the United States (Ariès 1962; Stone 1979; Shorter 1976; DeMause 1974). Age-graded common schools, orphan asylums, and children's aid societies all provided evidence for this contextual shift in ideological conceptions of childhood.[1]

The more proximate causes of this shift in statute, however, could be found, Zainaldin argues, in changes in judicial discretion in child custody disputes. There were, first, the cases in which judges for the first time began to explore the limits of their discretion in awarding custody. In a contest between a father of very little property and no house and a mother and maternal grandfather of some property and a house, the court, in *Nickols v. Giles* [2 Root 461 (Conn. 1796)], refused to grant the writ of *habeas corpus* brought by the father to regain custody of his child. *Commonwealth v. Nutt* [1 Bro. 143 (Philadelphia County Ct. C. P. 1810) pitted two parents of morally unwholesome character against one another, offering the judge little choice on any grounds but ones of precedent; the judge granted the fathers writ of *habeas corpus*. In the extremely colorful case of *Commonwealth v. Addicks* [5 Binn. 520 (Pa. 1813)], the mother admitted to marrying the man with whom she had committed adultery, thereby violating the laws of Pennsylvania. The father was denied custody, although three years later [*Commonwealth v. Addicks*, 2 Serg. & Rawl. 174 (Pa. 1816)] the judge granted the father custody, arguing that the children, now aged 9 and 13 had "arrived at a time in their life when their morals must necessarily be injured." That the mother originally was granted custody in spite of her admitted flagrant violation of the law was interpreted, however, as evidence that parenthood and childhood were being defined variously:

> In *Addicks* the court moved beyond *Nutt*, explicitly tethering the exercise of discretion to a conception of the child's interests. Sexual roles, parental conduct, the image of childhood, and the age of the child were becoming important components in the newly invented abstractions of "parental qualification" and "welfare of the child." The father's traditional common law claim to the custody of his legitimate child was being replaced by a vague but definite test for parenthood. (Zainaldin 1979, p. 1055)

Zainaldin claims that further evidence for these redefinitions can be found in cases in which the child's pecuniary interests take on importance. *In re Waldon* [13 Johns. 418, 419 (N.Y. 1816)], McGowan, the maternal grandfather of a young girl, was awarded custody (the mother had died in the interim), not because the father was shown to be in any way incompetent, but because the father had been insolvent and had lived with his mother. McGowan, on the other hand, was wealthy and had no heirs other than his granddaughter.

Despite these amendments to case law in custody, Zainaldin comments that "It would be forced to contend that American courts in the first third of the century ignored the rights of fathers and natural parents" (1059). Zainaldin remarks on the vigorous application of paternal preference in the 1830s.

The 1840s were a time of confusion in custody judgments, but also one in which a distinctive role for the courts in determining custody was rediscovered. Judges spoke of the child's welfare as the most important factor in determining custody, and this was followed by laws enacted to allow for judicial discretion in matters of custody. Furthermore, some courts took note of the equality of parental claims in custody.

For Zainaldin, the most important development was the emergence of a set of guiding principles for a test of child's best interest. There were four. First was the age of the child, or the so-called Tender Years Doctrine, arguing for the supremacy of the mother's care in the early years [*Mercein v. People ex rel. Barry*, 25 Wend. 65, 106 (N.Y. 1840)].[2] Second was the notion that boys of nontender ages should be placed with their fathers [*In re Gregg*, 6 Pa. L. J. 528, 534 (N. Y. City Super. Ct. 1847)]. Affective bonds and children's wishes,[3] when expressed, were the third and fourth principles. These, then, formed the linchpin upon which adoption (vesting of custody in a nonnatural parent) could be built. Zainaldin concludes:

> In short, the law of child custody in the new republic rested upon a developing conception of childhood and parenthood. The judiciary clearly appreciated the vulnerability of childhood. Judges also spied a subtler, more profound truth: character was formed through association. Habits and personality were molded by family environment. Thus, through the discretionary determination of custody, judges acted not only to preserve idyllic childhood, but also to promote an environment that would blend innocence with morality. The child was infinitely malleable, and if environment was important, nurture was critical. (1085)

In setting the stage for further research on the subject of changes in child custody laws in the United States (and elsewhere), Zainaldin offers three arguments: these changes are due to (1) a general change in the conception of childhood, and, thereby, parenthood, (2) a widening of sexual roles in domestic relations, and (3) the increasing importance of the child's best interest as a determining factor in disputed child custody outcomes. Before turning to the development of these three arguments and critically appraising them, Michael Grossberg's approach to this same change in American family law will also be considered.

Grossberg's Argument

Like Zainaldin, Grossberg (1985) draws on cases of the period to guide his inquiry into the change in parental presumption in custody disputes, and, like Zainaldin, this leads him to conclude that fathers lost their presumption to custody in the courts in the mid-1800s. Unlike Zainaldin, however, Grossberg attributes this change to forces beyond familial relations.

The first of these forces is the generally expanding legal rights of women, particularly those having to do with women's increasing control over property within marriage. Maternal custody became a possibility as the extent of their control over property increased. Children might be considered like property, and women could be given control of them. When states regulated women's control of property, husbands lost their rights to do so.

Thus, states' rights generally were increased, according to Grossberg, by extending the discretion of the judiciary. When judges had the right to make custody determinations, it was the state, in essence, that garnered parental power as its own. The greater the sphere of discretion, the greater the scope of state's rights: "The widespread desire to use the law to encourage proper family life led to statutory directives and judicial decisions that subjected parents and children to ever-tightening controls . . . [and] authorized the courts to weigh claims for children's interests against legal rules emphasizing household integrity and social stability" (p. 283).

Grossberg perceptively observes that the increase in women's rights (including their custodial rights) as well as children's rights to individual integrity within the family were given contingently. If there was to be "enlightened discretion" (Pomeroy 1892), it was to be exercised ultimately in the *state's* interest.

Despite his acknowledgment of the importance of the state's interests, Grossberg nonetheless locates the causes of the impetus toward women's and children's rights in realms quite separate from that of the state. Instead, changes in the legal orientation to women and children are seen to emanate from a growing concern with child nurture and the acceptance of women as more legally distinct individuals, with a special capacity for moral leadership and childrearing. This, in turn, could be traced to the increasing segregation of homebound women (see also Grossberg 1983).

The segregation of women was, for Grossberg (and others, see below), a new basis for their increasing legal clout: women used the newly enshrined domestic virtues as a justification for why their claims should be considered. If they were held to be the superior parent within marriage, then why not also at the time of its demise? Thus domestic powers—to be exercised independently of male leadership or control—were to be recognized by the courts.

Maidment's Argument

Maidment's (1984) argument for England's shift in presumptive custody has a slightly different focus. Like Zainaldin and Grossberg, she accords some of the cause to changing ideological conceptions of women and children within the family, but she also notes the efforts of activists in the passage of particular bills.

The ascendancy of the welfare principle was, for Maidment, attributable to three sources: increasing concern for the emotional welfare of the child, their improved record of physical survival, and improvements made on their behalf in health care, including the growth of pediatrics as a specialty and the development of hospitals for children. Yet, Maidment cautions, not too much credit should be awarded for the judicial expression of concern over children's welfare, for this was interpreted within the boundaries of status quo conceptions of marriage and family. Indeed, the appeal of the welfare principle to lawmakers may have been that it diverted attention from the issue of women's rights.

The recognition of joint guardianship of children, Maidment suggests, owes more to the fight of women for parental equality within marriage than to any child protection philosophy. Their fight grew out of the twin effects of increasing dependence of middle class women on their husbands together with their increased status and decision-making power within the family, especially with respect to their children.

After the Married Women's Property Act passed in 1882, women turned their attention to guardianship and custody. Not until activists changed their tactics from emphasizing the importance of equality in marriage to emphasizing the need for legal change to satisfy the welfare of children were they able to meet with any success.[4]

For Maidment, the origins of principles of equal parental rights during marriage and the child's welfare as the first and paramount consideration in custody cases are inextricably linked. The decline of the father's absolute rights was necessary for the rise in concern over children's welfare, but the latter grew less from a concern with the interests of the child, and more from the fight of women for equality of legal rights. The laws that resulted reflected a compromise between activist demands and Parliament's entrenched position against changes in fundamental family structure.

The Consequences for Custody of the
Motherhood–Childhood Link

Because it is such an important part of our everyday lives, we are steeped in the ideology of modern motherhood, and it is difficult to grasp that motherhood as we know it is a social invention, a product of social forces (just as modern fatherhood is). It is difficult to imagine that more than half of French urban mothers of the eighteenth century sent their infants to the countryside to be nursed by strangers, a kind of partial rejection (Bandinter 1981).[5] The notion of an inalienable tie between parent and child, particularly between mother and child, is of recent origin. It is even more recent than the idea of a natural tie between fathers and children, which now, of course, is lost.

The same forces that conspired to isolate the mother in the home also exerted a similar effect on children. Children were, in this cult of domesticity, much less valued for the unskilled labor they had contributed previously (Boris and Bardaglio 1983): "Children changed from property that men wanted to control to individuals who required a great deal of attention and training." At the same time, capitalism contributed to the general lengthening of the period of childhood (Boyd 1989). Childhood and adolescence would be distinct phases, each requiring time and sustained attention.

Children became important for the type of persons that they might become (Atkins and Hoggett 1984), a notion that presumably emanated from the fashionable emphasis on evolutionary conceptions: survival of the fittest favors superior children. The adult who will emerge could be seen in the child who was developing (Bernard 1974).

Further, the necessary socialization was deemed dependent on a certain kind of mechanism, one that was affective and generally emotionally based. The increased importance of psychological functioning and well-being added weight to the attention paid to the psychic development of children.

Indeed, new scientific studies of childhood became important in the development of the invention of modern motherhood. The sense that there might be an optimal design for child raising meant that socialization could not be left to the idiosyncratic preferences of individual parents (Smart 1989). This, combined with the notion that the task of a parent was to civilize a child, rather than break its will (Rothman 1978), and to nurture the child as a distinct person (Lasch 1983) meant that a more subtle, refined approach to parenting would be required. Fathers were busy elsewhere, so the task would be left to mothers.

These new attributes of childhood—the isolation of the child (along with the mother) in the home, the lengthening of the phase of childhood, the sense that there was an ideal in parenting to which parents could aspire, the notion that children had to be prepared in a careful way for their place in the world—all suggested that the previously circumscribed role of mother was inadequate. Motherhood would have to go from being a part-time occupation to a noble calling (Ehrenreich and English 1978).

Ultimately, however, the conception of motherhood would be subtly but powerfully transformed from the idea of a role, even a noble one, to an upholding of the natural order of things; in time the social forces that gave rise to the invention of motherhood would be forgotten. Instead, it would be argued that there existed a natural bond between mother and child that was uniquely different—and superior to—the bond between the father and child. This was not an unimportant difference: severing the connection between social context and parental role proscription would eventually come to confuse those who sought to draw a line of logic from parenting to custody law, and those who fought to understand the logic of the law of custody itself.

How was it possible that so fundamental a change occurred without much activism? Though there was not, in fact, much concerted action surrounding the change in child custody law, there was some.

The Efforts of Feminists

The late 1800s and early 1900s were characterized by feminist efforts in two areas: the increasing demands for married women's rights, and for suffrage (Smart 1989; O'Donovan 1985; Ursel 1986; Bland 1987; Backhouse 1981; Fineman 1989; Smart and Brophy 1985; Maidment 1984; Speth 1982; Brophy and Smart 1981). There is no question of this generally high level of activism. Yet there were considerable differences of opinion within the ranks of feminist activists on domestic issues. There were at least two general strands with respect to women's position in the nineteenth century (Conway 1982). One was concerned with increasing the rights and claims of women within their separate sphere, the home. The second was oriented toward weakening the boundaries circumscribing the separate sphere in order to seek equality in social, political, and economic activity. These have a bearing on whether feminist activism can be causally connected to changes in custody law.

Consider, for example, the split between single and married women with respect to suffrage (Bland 1987). The question arose as to whether married women should be included in the fight at all:

> Feminists were not in total agreement over the best tactics for tackling the married woman's predicament. For a start, the suffrage movement was divided over the question of whether or not married women should be included in a woman's suffrage bill. Although the championing of married women's suffrage was certainly a minority position (which had led in 1889 to the formation of the Women's Franchise League), the 1890s witnessed increased interest in the position of married women more generally. It appears that gains for the married woman were lagging somewhat behind those of her single sister. (Bland 1987, pp. 143–144)

The institution of limited suffrage in the United States, permitting women to vote on issues such as school board elections or other domestic issues, confused matters considerably. Some limited suffrage, such as that offered by the Massachusetts legislature, was certain to drive wedges among women's interests as a whole: in 1879 Massachusetts enacted a law offering to women over age 21 the right to vote for school boards should they be able to give evidence of residence, stand an educational test, pay a poll tax, and give evidence of taxable property.

Kentucky, as the first state to grant limited suffrage (in 1836), permitted widows with children of school age to vote for Trustees of the school board. In Louisiana, all tax paying women could vote on the issue of taxes (Anthony and Harper 1973). These and other state differences served to separate women on the basis of their status as property owners, tax payers, mothers of school aged children, widows, and so forth.

Second, there was the considerable controversy among feminists about the issue of divorce. Some were opposed altogether; others were opposed to marriage in the first place. Some opposed divorce without grounds; some opposed divorce with grounds (Livermore et al. 1890). (Activism regarding divorce laws will be taken up again in Chapter 5.)

Third, there could be no real consensus on the question of custody of children following divorce. On the one hand, the improvement of women's legal position within marriage and outside of it would not be complete without them having the right of custody or guardianship. On the other hand, however, there was a case to be made, on feminist grounds, for paternal custody. First, having custody would hamper women's ability to enter the labor force. Increasing access to higher status occupations was an important aim of at least single feminists, and they saw potential allies in the disproportionately middle and upper middle class divorced women. Second, it would cause special financial hardship for women; indeed, it might, in the long run, cause the immiserization of women. More conservative activists also worried that if paternal presumption were undermined, fathers' incentives toward their children prior to divorce might be altered in an untoward fashion. Thus, there was considerable dissension among women activists of this period regarding custody, divorce, and other related issues; there was no single voice even to oppose paternal presumption in custody.

Mostly, however, feminist concerns focused elsewhere. Reviewing evidence of activism surrounding the 1857 Divorce Act in England, Banks and Banks (1964, p. 52) note that

> Divorce had, to be sure, already been made easier. The Act of 1857 had opened up the way for the middle classes to emulate what their wealthier compatriots had been able to do since 1697. But . . . the feminists as such had been largely uninterested in the campaign which led to that Act and were equally uninterested in the amendments in the divorce law which occupied the next twenty years.

Since it was in these amendments that custody was delineated, feminists' voices were largely absent in this early formative period.

In the 1920s, however, Brophy (1982) finds evidence of direct participation of the National Union of Societies for Equal Citizenship on behalf of numerous women's societies in the crafting of the 1925 Custody of

Infants Act. In 1920 a bill was introduced on behalf of numerous women's societies that were concerned with the issues of guardianship, custody, and maintenance. This bill proposed that both parents should be joint guardians with equal rights and responsibilities instead of the father alone. In addition, an attempt was made to safeguard the custody and maintenance of children by allowing courts to make such orders while parents were living together.

The resistance that this bill faced was not so much a result of the rejection of the idea that women should have rights with respect to their children as it was a result of the sense that the provision would give women more power within marriage. Comments in the House of Commons debate suggested that this bill might deter men from marrying if they could not bring up their children as they wished, or it might lead to divorce for similar reasons.

Given this, some promoters refocused the debate on the issue of the need for such legislation to safeguard the interests of children (as opposed to its purpose of reducing inequality between men and women). Feminists came to argue that their demands for equality were not for their own sake but to protect the interests of children. Brophy (1982, pp. 158–159) writes about the struggle of the feminists and the Government:

> The Joint Select Committee had been convinced by the weight of evidence submitted by the Women's Societies that the custody law required change. Moreover, no case was made to the Committee which argued against the principle of equal rights to custody, and perhaps somewhat ironically, neither was it anticipated that the Courts would experience any difficulty in determining which parent was better suited to undertake this responsibility. The Committee therefore gave support to the demand for a change in the current law in relation to custody. However, it was somewhat illusory to allow a mother to claim custody of her children without giving her some means whereby she could support the children.

Yet, ultimately, the womens' societies split on the issue of what to do about demanding maintenance within marriage: the compromise arrived at ("Clause 3 Compromise") was that custody and maintenance were not enforceable if the woman was living with her husband. Brophy (1982, pp. 160–161) describes the tension:

> The feminist's response to this proposal was somewhat divided. The N.U.S.E.C. [National Union of Societies for Equal Citizenship] had, during this period, managed to secure provision in the Government's Bill to allow mothers equal rights with fathers to apply to the Courts in any matter regarding the children. This was . . . an important addition because it gave women a general right of application to the court. Even so,

there was considerable opposition to the compromise from many of the Women's Societies. There was some support for an outright rejection of the Government's Bill on the grounds that it left untouched crucial demands in the original Bill to alter power relations *within* the family. . . . The N.U.S.E.C., faced with a very real possibility that the Bill would indeed be lost, finally agreed to support the Government's measures.

Like other proponents of change in child custody, feminists came to mask their own interests with the cover of children's interests.

The Presumed Connection to Custody: Gathering the Strands of Explanation

These strands—the development of separate spheres, the cult of domesticity, and the invention of modern motherhood together with feminist activism—were combined into a logic supporting custody by the mother. Two new social facts—the separation of the father from the home and the declining economic value of children (and parenting)— had implications for fathering as a role. First, separation meant that the father's capacity to parent was curtailed. Furthermore, that separation led to a diminution of interest in fathering. Second, the lower the economic value of children, the less interested men were in their children. As men become less interested, women become more interested, aided by the increasing emphasis and value given to the role of mother.

If parenting was to be taken over by mothers in the context of marriage, then why not at the cessation of marriage? The idealization of motherhood, after all, had broken the hold of paternal right (O'Donovan 1979). And if children needed the care of their mothers in the context of marriage, would they not also require that care outside of the bonds of marriage? This reasoning led inexorably, it seemed, to the right of maternal custody following the cessation of marriage either due to death or divorce.

Were this the whole story, this chapter could end with the announcement that yes, indeed, the law changed in accordance with these new realities, and mothers were granted custody of their children following death and divorce. Yet, as we know from the previous chapter, *nowhere did the paternal right to custody give way to the maternal right to custody.* Instead, states everywhere took for themselves the rights that had previously belonged to fathers. Where, then, does the logic of these arguments fail?

Paternal–Maternal Equipoise

If the change in custody law had represented the substitution for one parent, the mother, for the other, the father, then seeking to understand why the mother suddenly became the preferred parent might have explained why custody law changed as it did. In fact, though, mothers and fathers were not substitutable either in the child's life or in the written law. (Their nonequivalence persists today.) Paternal–maternal equipoise was written into the law when the state took upon itself the ultimate responsibility of guardianship. Although Zainaldin himself ignores the implication of the following passage, he records it, nonetheless:

> Under the natural law, the senator [Paige] began, the father possessed no paramount right to the custody of his child. The wife and child were equal to the father, but inferior and subject to the sovereign. As husband and father, then, the male's authority was perfectly balanced by his wife's and child's, but in his capacity as sovereign family head the male was supreme. With the rise of civil society the father's sovereign power passed to the "chief or government of the nation." Naturally, the sovereign was not able to provide for all the children of the state and so transferred back to the parents the duty of education and maintenance and a right of guardianship. This delegation, though, was accompanied by an important limitation: sovereignty remained with the state. "The moment a child is born," the senator explained, "it owes allegiance to the government of the country of its birth, and is entitled to the protection of the government." The government in turn is obligated, by its duty of protection, "to consult the welfare, comfort and interests of such child in regulating its custody during the period of its minority." From this account of the rise of pre-civil society Paige concluded, first that there could be "no inequality between the father and mother" since parental rights derived from the "supreme power of the state"; and, second, that the state possessed an absolute and legitimate authority to interpose in parental disputes and determine custody. (Zainaldin 1978, p. 1071)

To interpret this equipoise as one of spirit—without making any reference to the state's role—is to fundamentally misinterpret the state of affairs in which paternal rights were assumed by the state.[6]

As for the obligations that defined parenthood so clearly, mothers and fathers could in no sense be considered substitutable. Though financial support had always been the bedrock of parental obligation, never were mothers expected to provide materially for their children, even though in the period of paternal presumption of custody, fathers had been expected to do so. Fathers' custodial rights had depended explicitly on their fulfillment of this obligation. Nor were custodial mothers expected to provide education for their children, as had been expected of custodial fathers.

Equality of men and women as parents, then, was equality before the state in its newly acquired and unhampered right to decide custody and guardianship. Equality of men and women as parents was achieved at an enormous cost: ceding the right of parenthood to the state. Mason (1994, p. 118) observes:

> Aggressive state actions designed to protect and promote children in this era finally demolished the fundamental common law relationship between parents and children, which had been only chipped at by nineteenth century courts. Never again would a father command absolute custody and control of his children.

This might have seemed draconian had it not been softened by the rhetoric that the state would take upon itself the burden of deciding the child's best interest.

The Rhetoric of the Best Interest of the Child

That the rhetoric of concern for the best interest of the child in custody disputes arose concurrently with the rise of motherhood and the removal of absolute paternal rights seemed to forge an unimpeachable relationship. In fact, it is nearly a classic case of a spurious one.

First, the welfare of the child was not a new concept, and neither was parental qualification. Both figured prominently, as we have seen in Chapter 2, in paternal right. Parental qualification was precisely why fathers had legal custody in the first place, and that qualification was defined in terms of the welfare of the child. The welfare of the child— the right to an education, to protection, and to material support—was itself the incentive given to the father to fulfill his obligations.

With the introduction of the state as a separate actor in questions of custody, achieved through the expansion of judicial discretion, the relationship between parental obligation and custody—and therefore that between parenting and children's welfare—was severed. By taking children's welfare as its own guiding principle, the state ensured that its right to decide would be inviolable. After all, children cannot speak for themselves. There is never any possibility of their collective action on their own behalf. And when they represent their interests privately, their representation is always open to question.[7] Thus, debates about what might constitute the child's best interest might go on indefinitely, but the issue *could never be decided* definitively. And precisely because parents' interests could be demonstrated to be separable from those of their children, especially upon divorce, the state could always retain its power to adjudicate such disputes.

It is worth remembering that women were never empowered as mothers as men previously had been empowered as fathers. This was in part as a result of their inability to provide for their children, an asymmetry that has its own history and explanation. In part, though, it was also because it was a time that the state took parental power away, not only from fathers, but from mothers as well, under the guise of concern for children, and in response to calls for equality. It was an equality of impoverishment of rights. Ultimately it would be the children of divorce who would be all the poorer.

One question that has rarely been posed is whether children—as separate from their mothers—were better or worse off under the regime of paternal presumption of custody. That this question is never asked is itself telling. The refusal to ask it comes from the entrenched idea that the presumption of custody would not have changed had children's interests not been served by such a change (an idea that I hope to have cast considerable doubt on by now). The answer to whether children were better off naturally depends on who the children were, and on what sorts of parents they had. Interestingly, the explanation for the change in custody that draws on the three strands of separate spheres, the withering of fathers' interests in their children, and the invention of modern motherhood, draws its imagery from wholly separate classes, though this remains largely unacknowledged by its authors.

Class Differences in Imagery

It is mistaken to think of the custodial rights of fathers as an unwelcome burden on their shoulders. Not only was there a presumption of paternal custody, but there was also a presumption that fathering was a most important—*the* most important—role in parenting. As has been noted previously, it was this set of parental obligations and feelings that provided the substance of the law of paternal custody itself. This is apparent, for instance, in an 1860 New Hampshire Court decision awarding a 10-year-old daughter to her father:

> The breaking of ties which bind the father and the child can never be justified without the most solid and substantial reasons. Upon the father the child must mainly depend for support, education and advancement in life, and as security for this he has the obligation of law as well as the

promptings of that parental affection which rarely fail to bring into service
of the child the best energies and the most thoughtful care of the father.

To communicate the essence of fatherhood of the 1700s, John Demos
(1986), the historian of early American families, calls on descriptors such
as pedagogue, benefactor, psychologist, moral overseer, example, pro-
genitor, companion, and caregiver. Correspondence (fathers, not mothers, corresponded with their children) and parenting books of the time,
which were primarily directed toward fathers, hardly give much cred-
ence to the notion of fathers interested only in the economic gain to be
had from the labor of their children.

Yet it will be properly objected that the fathers for whom correspondence has been recorded and to whom parenting books were addressed
are not the same fathers whose children were sent out to earn a wage.[8]
That is precisely the point. For a very long time, the children of the
classes beyond the middle class had failed to be an economic asset to
their parents. In fact, they were—as they are now—a considerable economic burden. Wrongful death suits demonstrated that the courts were
cognizant of this fact. In *Potter v. Chicago and Northwest Railway* [21 Wis
277 (1867)], the judge concluded: "The children of such parents receive
far more pecuniary aid . . . from their parents, than their parents from
them." So the notion that fathers lost interest in their children when
they were no longer of economic value is inconsistent with the documented evidence that fathers whose children were most likely to be a
burden were also those who evinced considerable interest in them. The
motivation for the change in child custody law cannot come from the
motives and feelings of the fathers themselves.

Second, the cult of domesticity was a predominantly middle-class
phenomenon: neither upper-class women nor working class women
were much taken by it (Badinter 1981). Middle-class women were, Bandinter (1981) notes, "the last women to give their children up and the
first to take them back." In contrast, aristocratic women were the first to
give up their children and the last to take them back. And the working
class simply could not afford such an expensive ideology. As Bose (1987)
notes perceptively, the domestic code served to sharpen class distinc-
tions among women. Thus, while the strand of the argument characterizing fathers derives from the reality of poor fathers' lives, the strand
of the argument characterizing mothers comes from the lives of the
middle class.

Finally, the children who were most at risk of being subject to the
changes in custody laws were most likely to be drawn neither from the
working nor the middle classes.

It would seem then that the story being told has a poor father, a middle-class mother, and an upper-middle-class child!

Concern with Incentives

Separate spheres for women and men and the change to a marked division of labor in marriage meant that the dissolution of marriage was no less momentous than it had been when the basis of marriage was a more multistranded affair. That it might have been accompanied by a greater emphasis on love as against social correctness could offer no salve to those concerned by the increasing divorce rate. Love might have been a good reason to marry, but it was also a good reason to divorce.

What would be the incentive for men and women to stay married to one another when their mutual affection had withered away? There were a variety of mechanisms available to the state to encourage marital solidarity. One of them was to tie blame in divorce suits to custody of children. Zainaldin notes that the wife's "marital obedience was becoming a prerequisite for custody" (1063). This is an interesting observation, for it is clearly an instance in which the state's interest in preserving marriage takes precedence over a concern for the welfare of the child. Certainly the argument could be mounted that a blameless father is a superior parent on moral grounds to a fallen mother, but using marital obedience to determine custody seemed better designed as a weapon in the state's arsenal to stem the rising tide of divorces than as a proscription for selecting a superior parent.

Returning to the Central Historical Question

Had custody law changed according to the logic emanating from the social forces that gave rise to separate spheres, the cult of domesticity, and the invention of modern motherhood, the law would have passed paternal rights and obligations to mothers. Maternal custody meant something entirely different than paternal custody, however, for it was expressly predicated neither on right, which was garnered by the state, nor on obligations, some of which remained with the father and some of which were relegated to the state.

Thus we must seek a different kind of logic. We still do not understand why men ceded control of their children while continuing to assume financial obligation to them. The critique of the argument beginning this chapter leads to several new kinds of questions, as well. What did the state have to gain by taking on the responsibility for determining child custody, other than an increase in its discretionary power? How did class differences in the probability of divorce enter into the change in custody law?

It was probably the case that the state was far more concerned with the consequences of the rising divorce rate than it was with the welfare of children. The problem of custody was but one of the problems that emanated from divorce. There were others, as well, not the least of which was what to do about the increasing numbers of divorced middle- and upper-middle-class women. It is to the increasing divorce rate that I now turn.

Notes

1.   An emphasis of the sexual role in domestic relations, as represented by the cult of "true womanhood," gave further impulse to the new adoption law, as well as general transformations in American family laws.

2.   Related cases include *State v. King*, 1 Ga. Dec. 93 (1841); *Commonwealth v. Maxwell*, 6 Mon. L. Rep. 214 (Mass. 1843); *Foster v. Alston*, 7 Miss. (6 How.) 406 (1842); *In re Gregg*, 6 Pa. L.J. 528 (N.Y. City Super. Ct. 1847).

3.   Cases upholding the importance of affective bonds included *Foster v. Alston*, 7 Miss. (6 How.) and *Ward v. Roper*, 26 Tenn. (7 Hum.) 1846. On the importance of the child's prerogative, see *Commonwealth v. Taylor*, 44 Mass. (3 Met.) 72 (1841).

4.   Maidment reports that activists—under different umbrella organizations including the National Union of Women's Suffrage Societies and the National Union for Equal Citizenship—introduced the idea of equal guardianship before Parliament every year for four years. Objections to their position were that equal rights would harm the father's position as head of the household, encourage domestic strife, and damage the consistent discipline of the child.

5.   Badinter (1981) notes that while this practice began in the thirteenth century, the demand for wet nurses grew so markedly in the eighteenth century that a shortage developed.

6.   This is also the solution to the riddle of adoption that Zainaldin poses. As long as paternal rights were understood as paramount, and as long as parental obligations stemmed directly from those rights, adoption could not be easily fit into the legal scheme. Yet once the state took those rights for itself, and doled out obligation as it saw fit, nonbiological parents—third parties—assumed relatively equal footing with parents themselves.

7.   Children can be consulted about what they wish to do, about what they see in their own best interests, but because they have such limited experience and time horizons, not to mention discipline, those wishes can always be overridden *in their best interests!*

8.   Nineteen percent of children aged 10–15 were at work in 1870, and they were found predominantly in the textiles, iron and steel, clothing, and lumber and furniture (Census figures, reported in Bremner 1971). In a study examining why it was that children worked, the reasons given were as follows: low wages and unemployment of parents, father's death, father's sickness, father's desertion of family, father's intemperance, father in prison, school difficulties, because friends went to work, to get better clothes, to enable parents to save, sickness of child while at school, and father's laziness (reported in Bremner 1971, p. 636).

4

The Pressure of the Rising
Divorce Rate

Divorce threatens children's security because it reduces the incentive of parents to contribute to their children. In a system of social organization in which the family disappears when marriage ends, divorce is the key threat to the security of children. Unlike adults, children have few, if any, alternative sources of material support, emotional support, and protection.

But the nature, type, and number of alternatives to the family available to adults varies. Particularly in the period of the late 1800s, women were more dependent on their marriages for material support than were men. This was true whether those women were also mothers or not. Jobs for middle- and upper-middle-class women were scarce, and remarriage was uncommon. It was these women, however, who had the greatest probability of divorce. Thus the increasing divorce rate had especially serious implications for middle-class women and their children.

Changes in legal institutions are commonly held to be brought about by a confluence of particular economic and political conditions that are specific to a sociolegal system. The extension of universal suffrage to all males regardless of race in the United States is one such example. Yet transformations in custody law took place in a large number of societies that had considerably different legal and political traditions, for example, civil law in one, common law in the other; a parliamentary system in one, a representative system in the other. That countries with such differences in conditions had similar outcomes suggests that the key causes of custody shift lay in generic social forces that, in their sweep, were little affected by national variations. What sorts of social forces might these have been that would have been sufficiently powerful to overcome these national differences?

Four pressures were mounting prior to and during the time that the change in custody occurred. These were the increasing divorce rate, the

59

increased number of children involved in divorces, the increased life expectancy for privileged white women, and the related decrease in maternal
and neonatal death rates. The first two pressures provide the subject matter for this chapter, and the last two the subject matter for Chapter 5.

The Importance of Divorce Rates for the Shift in Preference for Mothers over Fathers in Custody

When child custody became an issue because of divorce rather than
because of death, the fundamental character of the problem changed. In
the case of death there was no contest between parents—the child or
children were an obligation to be tended to, not a prize to be won or lost.
In the case of death either of the father or the mother, the remaining
parent could become an ally in sorrow instead of an adversary in love.

In Blackstone, questions about the custody of children were raised in
the event of the death of one parent. Upon the death of a mother—often
from the complications of childbirth—a father continued to retain custody of his children. Yet when a father died, custody could revert to a
number of different parties. On the one hand, common law clearly
insisted on the legal power of the father alone. On the other hand,
statute imposed the obligation to provide for children both on mothers
and on fathers. The father's obligation emanated, in the English case,
from his superior right and, in the American case, from his superiority
as a guardian. What basis there might be for the mother's obligation was
not clear: she had neither a right in the English case nor clear superiority
as a guardian in the American one.

Not surprisingly, then, English and American courts were of two
minds about awarding mothers custody following the death of fathers in
the 1800s. To some, this seemed a right stemming from nature: "The
father, and on his death the mother, is generally entitled to the custody
of the infant children, inasmuch as they are their natural protectors for
maintenance and education" (2 Kent Com., 205, 206). Yet others found it
much less obvious: "The mother is never considered as the guardian of
her children unless it be of nursed children till the age of seven years" (1
Swift Dig, 50). The courts could—and would—appoint a guardian in the
case of the father's death, with the father's wishes in this regard taken
into account. Typically, however, actual physical custody devolved to
the mother in the case of the father's death. Legal custody—control over
decisions regarding children's property and education—might go to the
mother but often to a court-appointed guardian, or to the state itself.

In no country did the law make the distinction between custody in the
case of death and custody in the case of divorce. Custody laws intended

to address a situation brought about by the death of a parent were applied directly to a situation brought about by the divorce of two parents. In some instances, particularly when the children were the objects of desire of both parents, the custody solution and the distributional problem were rather badly mismatched. Child support and visitation issues—not at all considerations upon the occasion of death—demanded ever more attention from courts.

The increasing divorce rate, therefore, meant more use of the custody laws on matters that could not have been envisioned by the authors of these laws. Custody law was well-suited to a situation characterized by two able and devoted parents. As more and more divorces involving more and more children came to the courts for resolution, the custody laws were extended to cover the multifarious terrain of family life.

Thus, the increasing divorce rate had numerous consequential effects for issues of child custody. First, as the number of divorces grew relative to the number of deaths, the nature of the application of custody laws changed fundamentally. Second, this increased divorce rate was expected to create a new potential welfare burden for states. Third, the increasing divorce rate would throw the security of children into serious question.

The State's Interest in Divorce

That states had an interest in marriage has been widely appreciated, and differences in state culture and ideology can be culled from the legal definition of marriage (Ames 1891). In Rome, marriage was conceived of as a contract based on consent. In postrevolutionary France, marriage was a social contract. American law made marriage a formal contract. In day-to-day married life, these differences might well have been lost— French and American wives might have found plenty of commonality for conversation—but recognition of the philosophical foundations of marriage meant that it was an institution that could be shaped. Following his comparative study of the history and development of Roman, Canonical, French, and German divorce legislation, Ames (1891, p. 1) remarked that

> In reality legal marriage is any thing which the legislator chooses to make it. It has any duties and rights which the law ascribes to it. It lasts exactly so long as the law holds it in force. . . . For there is no natural law—in marriage and divorce any more than in any other field of law.

It was not so far from this conception to propose that what could be created legally could also be dissolved, and that the conditions for dissolution could be controlled, as could the conditions for marriage. Yet marriage and divorce were not quite the same entities. In the first place, marriage had a long history—one could know from historical study the kinds of sociolegal experiments that had been successful. And, further, other institutions—particularly religious ones—could be expected to take a large part of the responsibility for fashioning marriage requirements.

In the second place, laws related to prohibitions against marriage of certain parties were fairly minimalist: only those marriages in which the states' interests were clearly contravened (such as interracial marriages in the antebellum United States), or in which the state was certain to become an unwilling partner eventually (because one of the parties was insane, for instance) were subject to extreme restrictions. The broadest marriage restrictions in all Western countries were levied against dependent youth. And the dependency of youth was a readily observable and easily documentable status characteristic.

Fashioning restrictions against divorce was to prove a much trickier problem. There was very little history on which to draw. In the sixth century, Justinian had allowed dissolution of marriage by mutual consent for a short time. Yet he coupled it with a penalty that those in the 1800s were unlikely to be willing to bear: one had to forfeit all property, be confined to a monastery for life, donate one-third of one's estate to the monastery, and donate the remaining two-thirds to one's children! In the 1800s, Japan had an exceptionally high divorce rate: in the period 1887 to 1898 the prevailing ratio was one divorce per three marriages. Following the introduction of the Japanese Civil Code of 1898, divorce in Japan became much more difficult to obtain.[1]

In addition to the dramatic evidence offered by the case of Japan, more ambiguous lessons came from a comparison of Belgium and France in the period of 1872–1881 (Walton 1913). During this period in Belgium both divorce and separation were allowed, and divorce by mutual consent was possible. Yet the divorce and separation rate was not significantly greater than it was in France, which had much more restrictive laws.

Price might be able to be used to control divorce. What was certain is that the expense of a divorce had a certain effect on its likelihood. In England of the mid-1800s, an undefended divorce cost from £60 to £250; a defended case cost from £250 to £5000. A renown judgment (by Justice Maule against a Mr. Thomas Hall, convicted of bigamy) in 1845 admitted this fact, tongue-in-cheek:

> Prisoner at the bar, you have been convicted before me of what the law regards as a very grave and serious offence: that of going thorough the

marriage ceremony a second time while your wife was still alive. . . . Another of your irrational excuses is that your wife had committed adultery. . . . The law in its wisdom points out a means by which you might rid yourself from further association with a woman who had dishonoured you; but you did not think proper to adopt it. I will tell you what that process is. You ought first to have brought an action against your wife's seducer if you could have discovered him; that might have cost you money, and you say you are a poor working man, but that is not the fault of the law. You would then be obliged to prove by evidence your wife's criminality in a Court of Justice, and thus obtain a verdict with damages against the defendant, who was not unlikely to turn out a pauper. . . . You must then have gone, with your verdict in your hand, and petitioned the House of Lords for a divorce. It would cost you perhaps five or six hundred pounds and you do not seem to be worth as many pense. But it is the boast of the law that it is impartial, and makes no difference between the rich and the poor. The wealthiest man in the kingdom would have had to pay no less than that sum for the same luxury; so that you would have no reason to complain. (quoted in Phillips 1988, pp. 416–417)

The evidence presented to the Royal Commission on Divorce and Matrimonial Causes in England presented to the Parliament on November 2, 1912 noted that "there is still practically one law for those who can afford to bring a suit in the Divorce Court and another for those who cannot, and the latter class embraces a very large portion of the population" (Royal Commission 1912, pp. 540–541). Even in the United States, the cheapest divorces varied in price from $50 in Connecticut to $2 in Indiana (Walton 1912).[2] The relation between cost and probability of divorce was graphically depicted by Willcox (1891, p. 3):

Imagine a society as a huge pyramid in which the position of each individual .is determined by his knowledge and wealth. Imagine a horizontal plane intersecting the pyramid to represent the divorce law of the community and all persons above the plane as possessing so much knowledge and money that divorce is to them a theoretical possibility, while to those below it is not. If the plane be motionless the rate of increase of divorce may be found; but if it be gradually sinking towards the base of the pyramid and making divorce a practical possibility to an increasing proportion of the whole number, this change must affect the calculation.

Religious tenets could, with some considerable bending, provide a guide. Divorce had always been possible for Jews, following a relatively complex ritual. Christians, though, were joined in marriage for life. Release from marriage might come, however, if one had offended a higher order law. The commandment against adultery seemed to be such a law.[3] In the United States between 1887 and 1906, 31.7% of divorces granted to husbands and 11.6% of divorces granted to wives listed adultery as the sole cause (U.S. Census Special Reports 1909). In England and Wales, 99.5% of the divorces granted to husbands were on the grounds of adultery alone (over half of the divorces were granted to husbands).

Except in South Carolina, where no divorce was permitted, adultery was a sufficient grounds for divorce, at least if the adultery was the woman's. States of the United States varied with respect to gender differentiation on grounds. According to English law of this period, simple adultery was grounds for a husband for an absolute divorce; for a wife, adultery was grounds only when accompanied by cruelty, desertion, or other aggravating circumstances.

The Sense of Urgency Occasioned by Rising Divorce Rates

From the present vantage point in which it is routine to discuss the statistic that 60% of first marriages are likely to end in divorce, the divorce rate of the turn of the century seems a mere snag in the social fabric. Table 4.1 shows the number of divorces from 1890 to 1920 in various countries. In 1920, the United States gained the dubious distinction of having the highest divorce rate in the world; by 1890 it had the highest divorce rate of any Western country. Nonetheless, it is not the absolute numbers that are so remarkable, but the rate of change. In 1890 there were 53 divorces per 100,000 people; by 1920, there were 139 per 100,000. The rate of change is even more remarkable in other countries. France's rate went from 17 divorces to 71 per 100,000 in the same period of time. Germany's change in rate from 13 to 63 per 100,000 was quite similar to the change observed in France. Switzerland, a leader among Western countries in divorce in 1890, had a more modest change than other countries: from 30 to 51 per 100,000. England had one of the greatest rates of change: from 1 per 100,000 in 1890 to 17 per 100,000 in 1920. These changes were striking enough to catch the attention even of those who were not given to routine social observation.

It is possible to get another kind of sense of the increasing divorce rate by considering the change in the number of marriages per divorce in just the short period from 1867 to 1886. Consider Table 4.2. In 1867 in Belgium there were 294 marriages per divorce; by 1886 that number had been cut by more than half, to 112. In France, the change was equally dramatic: 138 marriage for every divorce were recorded in 1867 but by 1886 there were but 46 marriages for each divorce. In England and Wales the number of marriages registered per divorce was divided by nearly a third in those 20 years. These statistics comprised what was known, fearfully, as the divorce problem.

Table 4.1.   Divorces per 100,000 Population

Country	1880	1890	1900	1910	1920
United States	38	53	73	92	139
Japan		269	143	113	94
France		17	25	37	71
Germany		13	15	24	62
Switzerland	33	30	32	43	51
Belgium	3	6	11	14	49
Holland	4	8	10	16	29
Sweden	5	6	8	11	21
Australia		6	10	12	19
England and Wales	1	1	2	3	17

Source: Adapted from U.S. Census, Special Reports, Marriage and Divorce, 1867–1906.

Divorce in the United States, 1867–1920

Divorce Rates and Laws in the United States

Divorce Rates

In 1867, 9937 divorces were granted in the United States. By 1900, that number had grown to 55,751, and by 1929, to 201,468. The dramatic increases are evident in Table 4.3, showing the increases in divorces by 5-, 10-, and 20-year periods. Nearly 20 times the number of divorces were granted in 1926 as in 1867.

How dramatic were these differences, in fact? An answer to this question comes from a consideration of divorces relative to the population as a whole, and the married population more specifically, both of which also showed marked growth. Table 4.4 compares the increase in population with the increase in divorce from 1875 to 1925 in 5 year intervals.

Table 4.2.   Number of Marriages per Divorce for 1867, 1876, and 1886

Country	1867	1876	1886
Belgium	294	191	112
France	138	115	46
England and Wales	1378	859	527
Netherlands	225	178	72
Sweden	199	147	133
Switzerland	—	20	22
United States	1233	935	676

Table 4.3.   Divorces by 5-, 10-, and 20-Year Periods in the United States

Year	Number/5 years	Number/10 years	Number/20 years
1922–1926	841,165	1,550,595	2,460,460
1917–1921	709,430		
1912–1916	504,507	909,865	
1907–1911	405,358		
1902–1906	332,642	593,362	945,625
1897–1901	260,720		
1892–1896	194,939	352,263	
1887–1891	157,324		
1882–1896	117,311	206,595	328,716
1877–1881	89,284		
1872–1876	68,547	122,121	
1867–1871	53,574		

The percentage increase in population never reached even half the percentage increase in divorce. As the population grew dramatically, from nearly 40 million in 1870 to over 100 million in 1925, the incidence of divorce grew even more: where there had been a divorce rate of 0.27 (per 1000 population) in 1870, by 1925 that rate had grown to 1.55.

The married population was also growing rapidly, though not as dramatically as either the population itself or the divorced population. Here, too, the divorce rate led, so much so that in the period from 1870

Table 4.4.   Total and Percentage Increase of Population and of Divorces Compared, 1870–1925

Year	Population		Divorces		Population to one divorce	Divorces per 1000 population
	Total	Increase (%)	Annual average	Increase (%)		
1925	114,242,833	8.1	176,887	20.0	646	1.55
1920	105,710,620	6.5	147,336	38.5	718	1.39
1915	98,841,443	7.5	106,351	25.7	929	1.07
1910	91,972,266	9.5	84,621	24.8	1,087	0.92
1905	83,983,420	10.5	67,791	22.1	1,239	0.81
1900	75,994,575	9.4	55,502	36.7	1,369	0.73
1895	69,471,144	10.3	40,612	22.3	1,711	0.58
1890	62,947,714	11.3	33,197	34.8	1,896	0.53
1885	56,551,748	12.7	24,624	28.6	2,297	0.44
1880	50,155,783	11.5	19,143	33.2	2,620	0.38
1875	44,987,116	13.0	14,369	28.2	3,131	0.32
1870	39,818,449	—	11,207	—	3,553	0.27

Sources: Adapted from U.S. Census, Marriage and Divorce 1916, 1922–32.

Table 4.5.   Percentage of Divorces to Wives, by State

Under 50%	More than 66%
North Carolina	Pennsylvania
Mississippi	Arizona
Alabama	Colorado
Virginia	Wisconsin
South Carolina	Nebraska
Florida	Iowa
West Virginia	Minnesota
	Wyoming
50%–66%	Illinois
Georgia	Vermont
Arkansas	Kansas
Texas	Massachusetts
Utah	Michigan
Louisiana	Connecticut
Dakota	Maine
Kentucky	Indiana
Maryland	Washington
Tennessee	Washington D.C.
Delaware	Ohio
New York	Oregon
New Jersey	Idaho
Missouri	Utah
New Mexico	Montana
New Hampshire	California
	Rhode Island
	Nevada

to 1920 there was more than a four-fold increase in the divorce rate, as computed to the married population, from 0.81 to 3.41.

Divorce rates did differ by state. In 1870 the rates ranged from 3 per 100,000 in South Carolina to 611 per 100,000 in Nevada. By 1880 South Carolina, with its prohibition against divorce, remained the state with the lowest rate, but Colorado had the distinction of being the state with the highest divorce rate (781 per 100,000). These differences can be seen in Table 4.5. Some of the variation appears related to geographic divisions, but there are many exceptions. Still, there is a rough parallel of divorce rate by region—Atlantic, Central, and Pacific—with the New England states the exception to the generally lower divorce rate in the Atlantic division.

If instead we consider the percentage of divorces given to wives across states, another geographic division becomes evident: Southern states were less likely to grant divorces to wives than to husbands in the 1870s and 1880s, in contrast to states elsewhere (see Table 4.5). Though eventually the balance of divorces would shift so that more wives were

Table 4.6. Percentage of Divorces Granted to Husbands and Wives, 1867–1929

United States and geographic divisions	1919		1922		1916		1887–1906		1867–1886	
	To husband	To wife	To husband	To wife	To husband	To wife	To husband	To wife	To husband	To wife
United States	28.7	71.3	32.0	68.0	31.1	68.9	33.4	66.6	34.2	65.8
New England	26.4	73.6	27.4	72.6	25.9	74.1	28.2	71.8	29.3	70.7
Middle Atlantic	30.4	69.6	36.7	63.3	33.0	67.0	33.7	66.3	35.6	64.4
East North Central	26.3	73.7	29.0	71.0	27.4	72.6	27.0	73.0	29.9	70.1
West North Central	25.3	74.7	28.7	71.3	27.6	72.4	30.4	69.6	33.0	67.0
South Atlantic	33.6	66.4	37.9	62.1	38.8	61.2	46.9	53.1	49.2	50.8
East South Central	33.5	66.5	37.5	62.5	38.2	61.8	45.8	54.2	46.0	54.0
West South Central	33.0	67.0	35.6	64.4	38.0	72.0	42.0	58.0	45.5	54.5
Mountain	29.6	70.4	30.9	69.1	29.5	70.5	28.0	72.0	35.4	64.6
Pacific	24.1	75.9	28.5	71.5	26.0	74.0	27.4	72.6	25.5	74.5

Table 4.7. Urban and Rural Rates of Divorce, U.S.

District	Divorces, annual average per 1000 population			
	1900	1890	1880	1870
States having city counties	0.69	0.51	0.39	0.31
City counties	0.72	0.53	0.44	0.34
Other counties	0.68	0.51	0.38	0.31

granted divorces in all states and regions than husbands were, the pattern whereby wives would be granted relatively fewer of those divorces in the South held throughout the 1920s. Table 4.6 shows that in the South Atlantic, East South Central, and West South Central regions, husbands were still being granted one-third of all divorces. This is especially interesting in light of the progression by which states adopted statutes formally recognizing mother's equal parental rights: as shown in Table 2.1, Southern states were consistently among those that adopted such laws later—after 1922—rather than earlier.[4]

In addition to comparing divorce rates by region, divorce rates in urban and rural areas may be compared. Despite the common view that urban divorce rates were greatly in excess of those in rural areas, in fact, the differences are quite modest. Table 4.7 shows, for example, that in city counties in 1870, the average number of divorces per 1000 population was 0.34 in city counties whereas for other (noncity) counties, the rate was 0.31. In 1900, the rates were 0.72 for city counties and 0.68 for others. Some cities did contribute more than their share to their state's overall divorce rate. Denver is among the most dramatic: though its population comprised but 27.5% of the state's total, and 26.0% of the state's marriages, it contributed 40.7% of the state's divorces in the period 1867–1906. Other cities with a strikingly disproportionate share of their state's divorce rates included Baltimore and Chicago. Yet there were more examples in which the percentage of divorces did not outstrip the percentage of the population by very much—San Francisco, New Orleans, St. Louis, Philadelphia, and Cleveland—and one—New York City—in which the percentage of divorces was actually lower than the percentage of the population that the city contributed to the state.

Children Affected by Divorce

Table 4.8 reports the party to whom the divorce was granted, by state, and the person to whom custody of the children ultimately was granted. These data are marred by considerable variations in failure to report about the status of the children. The numbers contained within the table

Table 4.8. Who Gets the Divorce and Who Gets the Children, by State, 1887–1906

State or Territory	Granted to husband				Granted to wife			
	Total	With children (%)	No children (%)	% DK	Total	With children (%)	No children (%)	% DK
Alabama	13,093	5.8	18.7	76.0	9,714	16.5	17.6	65.9
Arizona	795	28.8	63.1	8.1	1,585	50.1	46.1	3.8
California	6,409	33.7	54.0	12.4	18,761	52.4	39.3	8.3
Colorado	4,493	28.8	45.8	25.4	11,351	45.6	35.1	19.3
Connecticut	2,730	18.2	61.0	20.8	6,494	44.6	40.9	14.3
Delaware	311	13.8	6.8	79.4	576	24.1	5.6	70.3
D.C.	633	42.2	32.9	25.0	1,692	54.9	26.5	18.6
Florida	3,707	15.7	11.8	72.5	3,879	33.7	9.4	56.9
Georgia	4,759	21.2	41.4	37.4	5,642	35.3	35.8	28.9
Idaho	956	35.7	62.8	1.6	2,249	55.4	42.3	2.3
Illinois	22,474	30.2	64.1	5.7	59,735	50.3	45.6	4.0
Indiana	16,360	27.7	56.5	15.8	44,361	47.8	40.8	11.3
Iowa	8,490	31.1	49.2	19.8	26,384	54.3	31.9	13.8
Kansas	8,544	30.0	37.7	32.3	20,360	52.3	27.0	20.8
Kentucky	12,559	14.6	38.5	46.9	18,082	36.3	29.8	33.9
Louisiana	4,702	17.3	44.2	38.6	5,083	29.6	40.8	29.6
Maine	3,804	29.4	49.2	21.4	10,390	48.4	35.4	16.2
Maryland	2,896	41.5	50.1	8.4	5,024	53.8	39.8	6.4
Massachusetts	6,732	21.0	25.8	53.1	16,208	39.0	20.1	40.9
Michigan	11,574	45.1	53.7	1.2	30,824	57.2	42.0	0.8

State								
Minnesota	4,192	40.1	48.9	11.0	11,454	56.9	35.2	8.0
Mississippi	11,674	6.9	53.2	39.9	8,319	16.4	45.9	37.6
Missouri	18,815	22.7	46.1	31.2	35,951	44.6	33.8	21.6
Montana	1,688	26.1	56.0	17.9	4,766	48.1	39.8	12.1
Nebraska	4,626	29.2	51.6	19.2	12,088	52.1	36.4	11.4
New Hampshire	2,785	22.5	6.7	70.8	5,832	44.2	4.9	50.8
New Jersey	2,720	45.2	49.5	5.3	4,721	60.6	36.5	2.9
New Mexico	798	30.7	64.8	4.5	1,639	48.7	48.3	2.9
New York	10,103	45.0	53.1	1.9	19,044	51.0	46.8	2.2
North Carolina	4,103	8.7	26.1	65.2	2,944	23.9	20.8	55.3
North Dakota	1,772	41.8	53.9	4.3	2,545	56.0	41.1	2.9
Ohio	17,260	39.0	52.8	8.3	46,772	53.3	40.2	6.5
Oklahoma	2,834	29.0	63.1	7.9	4,835	49.7	45.0	5.3
Oregon	3,943	39.1	57.8	3.0	7,002	53.5	45.1	1.4
Pennsylvania	12,933	39.9	45.6	14.5	26,753	54.7	33.9	11.4
Rhode Island	1,517	19.4	80.3	0.3	5,436	40.9	58.7	0.4
South Carolina	—	—	—	—	—	—	—	—
South Dakota	2,782	40.2	49.6	10.2	4,326	55.0	38.5	5.5
Texas	24,895	12.6	51.7	35.7	37,760	32.1	39.8	28.1
Utah	1,050	35.1	57.8	7.0	3,620	58.0	39.0	3.1
Vermont	1,338	21.4	11.9	66.7	3,402	50.0	8.3	41.7
Virginia	6,318	252.6	37.1	37.3	5,811	44.7	28.7	26.7
Washington	4,571	37.6	60.2	2.2	11,644	50.6	47.6	1.8
West Virginia	4,731	28.9	33.0	38.1	5,577	43.4	26.9	29.8
Wisconsin	5,931	41.7	48.9	9.4	16,936	57.5	36.2	6.3
Wyoming	568	34.5	51.9	13.6	1,204	50.2	41.3	8.5

Source: U.S. Bureau of the Census, Marriage and Divorce, 1867–1906.

can therefore be compared in only the most general fashion. Nonetheless, comparisons within states can be telling, for in these it is safe to assume that the failure to report about the status of children in cases where divorces were granted to husbands occurs at the same rate as the failure to report about the status of children in cases where divorces were granted to wives.

In Arizona, for instance, among those divorces granted to husbands, slightly more than one-quarter had children, yet among those divorces granted to wives, fully half had children. In divorces granted to husbands in Illinois, with one of the highest divorce rates during this period, 30% had children, and half of those granted to wives had children affected by the divorce. In North Dakota however, which was characterized by one of the lower divorce rates of this time period, 40% of the divorces granted to husbands and 56% of the divorces granted to the wives involved children.

Children, then, were very much a part of the divorces of the time. Among those who divorced, having children seemed not to be a terribly strong deterrent. In 20 states, 30% or more of the divorces granted to husbands involved children. In 40 states, 30% or more of the divorces granted to wives involved children.

The average number of children per divorce in this period hovered around two. This is in part due to the average length of marriage before divorce. The average period between marriage and divorce ranged by state from just over 6 years in Arkansas and Tennessee to 12 years in Massachusetts. Divorce laws of the various states are relevant here. A large part of the explanation for Massachusetts' greater average period before divorce must be due, in large part, to the requirement that a spouse be deserted for 5 or more years before desertion could serve as a grounds for divorce. The average in the vast majority of states was either just over 8 or just over 9 years. Lichtenberger (1931), however, notes that the average length of marriage before divorce seemed to increase, rather than decrease, as might be expected. On average, therefore, children were relatively young at divorce. Women and men were too.

Cause of Divorce and Custody of Children

In the early period of the transition, the cause of divorce was quite relevant to the assignment of custody of children. This was because these causes established the grounds for fault, and fault could then serve as the basis for the assignment of custody. In the absence of a clear legal or philosophical bent toward one parent, fault was as good as any other guide; lofty ethical rationales for why these two ought to be tied were easily summoned. Only later would more sophisticated arguments that separated the impulses necessary for marriage from those necessary for parenting be advanced.

Table 4.9 enumerates the causes registered for divorces in which children were involved, by year. Desertion, adultery, and cruelty were consistently the most often classified causes: these were also the most often allowed causes in each state. In all but seven states, desertion was the most frequently cited cause for divorce where children were involved; in Louisiana and Maine, adultery was the cause most often registered; in Indiana, Missouri, Nevada, New Hampshire, Texas, and Vermont, cruelty bested desertion and adultery.

These grounds were not equivalent, however, in their apportionment among husbands and wives or among divorcing mothers and fathers. As the number of grounds for divorce grew, so did the gender differentiation in fault. The two most common causes, adultery and abandonment/ desertion, differ least between wives and husbands. By comparison, cruelty is cited much more often in divorces granted to wives than in those granted to husbands. Divorce cases where adultery was named as the cause and where there were children affected by the decree were almost evenly split between those granted to husbands and those granted to wives.[5] Thus, in states where only adultery was recognized as cause for divorce, as in New York for instance, the distribution of divorces granted to husbands and wives is much more even (for those with children, 45% to husbands, 51% to wives; for those without children, 53.1% to husbands, 46.8% to wives[6]). In contrast, the distribution of divorces among men and women in the state of Washington—where the law allowed cruelty, fraud, incapacity to contract marriage, indignities, intemperance, lack of real consent to marriage, neglect to provide, and any cause deemed sufficient by the courts—was much more pronounced in its unevenness (for those with children, 37.6% were granted to husbands, and 50.6% to wives). New York, in 1930, was one of the last states to enact a custody law that recognized the equal rights of mothers following divorce; Washington had already passed such a law 8 years before.

Considered from another point of view, we can ask whether husbands or wives were more likely to be granted the divorce on the relatively more gender-neutral grounds of adultery and desertion when no children were involved. Posing the question in this way we find that more than half the states granted more than half the divorces to husbands.[7] When there were children involved, and adultery was the named cause, again, more than half the states granted more divorces to husband than to wives.[8]

The second source of the association between the number and types

Table 4.9. Causes Cited in Divorces in the United States, 1887–1903, by Whether Children Were Involved

Cause cited	Granted to	Children[a]: numbers of divorces	No children: numbers of divorces
Adultery			
1887	H	859	1297
	W	872	757
1893	H	1117	1742
	W	1195	967
1898	H	1290	2107
	W	1322	1320
1903	H	1563	2679
	W	1705	1699
Desertion			
1887	H	1135	2216
	W	2895	2259
1893	H	1431	2881
	W	3818	2988
1898	H	1879	3811
	W	4575	3881
1903	H	2480	5222
	W	6188	5594
Cruelty			
1887	H	264	285
	W	2271	1381
1893	H	386	497
	W	3359	2238
1898	H	583	796
	W	4513	3133
1903	H	827	1319
	W	5825	4706

[a] Children affected by decree.
[b] H, husband; W, wife.

of causes and the change in child custody law lies in the relation these implied between the legislature and the judiciary. The more restricted the number of causes, the greater the power of the legislature relative to the judiciary in determining the character of divorce—and, thereby, custody arrangements—in a given state.[9] The transfer of power from the legislature to the courts in matters of divorce hastened the consideration of a new law for parental presumption in custody awards, precisely because of the gender imbalance implied by the increase in the number of causes. When it was in the province of the courts to decide on assignment of cause in divorce, divorces were more likely to be granted to the woman, and children were less likely to be assigned to the custody of their father. It is not, then, that courts were deciding on custody so much as they were deciding on fault, fault being the grounds upon which custody decisions increasingly depended.

Taken together, these were substantial changes. Some sense of the reaction they prompted can be culled from the transcripts of the debate around the Uniform Marriage and Divorce Act.

Debates about the Divorce Problem and
Its Implications for Children

Nearly every year for more than 25 years between 1894 and 1925, a bill called the Uniform Marriage and Divorce Act was introduced in the U.S. Congress,[10] and every year, it was defeated. The bill would have given the federal government power to regulate marriage and divorce. Presumably it would have regulated custody of children as well, although the custody of children was not, interestingly, a major part of the reform proposals incorporated in the Uniform Marriage and Divorce Act.[11] It is hard to believe the minuscule role that concerns about children played. To gain some idea, consider that in the 1906 Proceedings of the National Congress on Uniform Divorce Laws—a transcript that was 156 pages long—only slightly more than four pages were devoted to a discussion of Section 20, which was to require that

> No decree of divorce, interlocutory or final, shall be granted in any divorce suit in which there are minor children, until due and timely notice of the pendency thereof and the hearing thereon shall have been given to the prosecuting attorney, county attorney or other disinterested attorney appointed by the court of the county in which the proceedings are pending, and.a reasonable opportunity afforded to appear and represent the interests of such minor children. (Proceedings 1906, p. 119)

Senator Adolph Sloman of Michigan offered a defense of the amendment in the following terms:

> Now, it has been said here repeatedly that the State is party to the marriage and party to a divorce; and the State is interested very largely in the welfare of the minor children, who are likely to become either a public charge, or are likely to be placed in the custody of one or the other of the parties who is ill suited to look after their welfare . . . It is assumed that the court of chancery, which is supposed to be the guardian of minor children, would ordinarily attend to that, but it is absolutely impossible, in the numerous divorce cases presented to the court, for the court in the little time it might have, or with the parties simply before it, to inquire fully in to the situation and circumstances of those children. (Proceedings 1906, p. 120)

Opponents objected that courts were already much concerned with the interests of children, and, further, that, procedurally, such a provision would be cumbersome. In the words of Vice-Chancellor Emery (of New Jersey):

> The court exercises the powers of a court of chancery, which includes the oversight or special protection to the children. I think that it was the idea in the preparation of this final report, to eliminate, as far as possible, everything which might thereafter supplied by special provisions as to procedure. (Proceedings 1906, p. 121)

To those who did not appreciate how limited the state's interest in children's welfare really was, the outcome of the vote on this section would come as a surprise—it failed.

General concerns about the family and children were, however, expressed in the debates. Representative Norris, a Republican from Nebraska, stated that "The legitimacy of children, the rights of property, as well as the morality of society are all concerned and all involved in this question" (1911). Two years later, Senator Ransdell, a Democrat from Louisiana, argued that "The inevitable trend of divorce is to break up more homes than it builds up, and to materially reduce the number of children born. When marriage is dissolved, the true home ceases to exist, the parents and children are separated and the sweet ties that bind father and mother to their offspring and to each other are broken forever" (1913–1914). In 1915, Representative Raker from California spoke of the harm that divorce brings to children, and called such children "divorce-orphaned." He spoke of the figure of 1,689,662 divorces from 1867–1915 as the "call of the children" for a federal marriage and divorce law.

Raker, as well as various religious leaders, also made their voices heard on this issue. Divorce was dishonorable and would take "away the children's glory forever." He called upon his fellow legislators to "Help save the children from the blight of this consuming flame," and in this exhortation he was joined by Margaret Ellis of the Women's Christian Temperance Union.

Others spoke to the state's direct interest in marriage and divorce. In 1892 Senator Kyle, a Mississippi Democrat delivered a speech in which he spoke of marriage as a civil contract with the state:

> It is both moral and civil in its aspect . . . it is a contract . . . essential to society while the relations of husband and wife, parent and child to which it gives rise are the foundations of many rights acknowledged the world over. But it differs from other contracts in that the rights, duties, and obligations arising from it are not left entirely to be regulated by the

agreements of the parties but are to a certain extent matters of municipal regulation. . . . As a civil institution, the legislative powers must throw around it safeguards and regulation. (U.S. Congressional Record, 1892, Session 52–1, p. 790)

Several years earlier, in 1887, Senator Dolph, an Oregon Republican had expressed similar sentiments:

Because society so greatly suffers when the family relation is disrupted, the home destroyed, and the security lost which the family affords for the support, education, and training of the offspring of the marriage for useful members of the community, free and easy divorce is destructive of good government and morality, debasing the estimate which society places on the marital relation and is degrading to women. (U.S. Congressional Record, 1887, Session 50–1, p. 166)

In essence, the Uniform Marriage and Divorce Act as a whole was defeated not for any issues related to marriage and divorce but because it represented too radical a shift away from states' rights. This disjuncture confused some social observers. One noted that

The American people are divided on matters pertaining to divorce. Those opposed to any divorce, that carries the legal right of remarriage during the life time of the divorced husband or wife, sometimes combine with those urging the fewest legal causes of divorce, and the coalition presents a unified front against the exponents of "the open door" in divorce legislation. (Carrigan 1911, quoted in Katz 1974, p. 126)

Marriage and divorce laws had always been the province of the states. Although it was defeated at a national level and incorporated into the law of only three states by 1923, the transcripts of the debate around the bill offer a glimpse into the perceptions of lawmakers as to the possible causes and consequences of the increasing divorce rate.

Even if the number of divorces was still small, the rate of change was not. The rate of change was duly noted by one

lawmaker favorable to the Uniform Marriage and Divorce Act: The growing instability of the marital relation and the home has become a matter for grave social concern. . . . There is an essential need for the proposed legislation. Present conditions are a menace to the home and the welfare of society. Divorce has increased inordinately. It has increased 500 per cent in the last twenty years. . . . Too easy divorce is leading to moral deterioration. There is a growing loss of feeling for the sanctity and permanency of the home. The break-up of homes affect large numbers of children adversely. Eighty thousand children each year, or nearly two million children in twenty years, most of them under ten years of age are deprived of one

or both parents. Eighty per cent of child criminals are victims of divorce
conditions and come from broken homes. (Johnsen 1925)

Although this lawmaker's statistical calculations are suspect, the rapidly growing rate of divorce was of substantial concern to those contemplating the likely social consequences. Note also that the mention of
children in the quotation above refers only diffusely to the negative
effects on children ("The break-up of homes affect large numbers of
children adversely"), but specifically to the social problem for which the
state must take responsibility ("Eighty per cent of child criminals are
victims of divorce conditions"). This means that we must turn our attention to divorce.

Divorce in France

In the case of the United States, it is the variation in marriage and
divorce laws across the geographic expanse that deserves comment, but
in the case of France, it is the variation in marriage and divorce laws
across time. In French law separations had long been convertible into
divorces. In the original text of Article 310 of the Napoleonic Civil Code
of 1803 the relevant provision read as follows: "When a separation,
pronounced for any other cause than the adultery of the wife, has lasted
three years, the spouse who was originally the defendant may apply to
the Tribunal for a divorce, which shall be granted unless the spouse
originally plaintiff, being present or duly cited to appear, immediately
agrees to the cessation of the separation" (quoted in McIlwraith 1917).
Divorce was abolished, however, by the restored monarchy in 1816,
and not reinstated in the Civil Code until 1884.[12] Its reinstatement was
marked by considerable controversy, largely on religious grounds. Despite the controversy, the law nearly had the distinction of being as
modern as twentieth-century law: the Chamber of Deputies and the
Senate originally considered an amendment in which both parties
would have been able to claim divorce as a *right* after a period of 3 years
(McIlwraith 1917). The Senate, however, ultimately reversed its vote.[13]
The result was a compromise with the Chamber in which a conversion
following three years was possible, and ultimately rested with the discretion of the Court. Thus, the law was much like the law of 1816, except
that it no longer singled out the adulterous wife for special treatment.
This was not, however, the end of the matter of divorce. In 1893, one
of the deputies of the Chamber (M. Jullien) managed to have an amendment passed, providing that all final judgments of separation should be
convertible on the demand of one of the parties. Yet the Senate found
this too far reaching, and would agree only to make conversion obliga-

tory when the party who had originally obtained the separation made application for conversion. In 1906 the debate was once again revived.

The substance of the debate was remarkably like that of the debate in the U.S. Congress that was ostensibly about the centralization of marriage and divorce laws. Those who argued for automatic conversion were persuaded that the law could not right what had already been put asunder by an unhappy spouse, and, if it could not encourage a marriage, it should release the two from their state of marital limbo.[14] Further, these people claimed, separating and divorcing spouses were left to the vicissitudes of the idiosyncracies of individual judges; discretion ought to be replaced by uniformity.

Those opposed focused their concerns on the implications for the solidarity of marriage and the family. Separation and divorce were becoming too easily obtained; soon France would find itself replete with *les unions libres*. Contrary to those who found judicial discretion to be capricious, these proponents found judicial discretion to be fundamentally the humanitarian way. Finally—and unlike their foes—they expressed a general concern with the possible jeopardy that children might find themselves in were divorce so automatically acquired.

Those in favor of the new bill held the day, however, and the law was passed in the Chamber (379 to 169). Thus, the French law was the forerunner to the English bill of the same character, and followed the German Civil Code of 1878 that stated: "If judicial separation has been granted, either spouse may apply for divorce, by virtue of the decree for separation, unless, since the issue of such decree, conjugal relations have been resumed. Separation is granted on the same grounds as divorce and may at any time and on the demand of either party, be transformed into divorce." Just what effect these changes would have on children was left unspecified.

The effects of the vicissitudes of law are evident in the figures reported in Table 4.10. Divorces were allowed from 1803 to 1816, but after 1816, only separations were permitted until 1884, after which both divorce and separation were permitted. The window of opportunity afforded by the enactment of the law permitting divorce in 1803 is evident in the figure of 229 marriage to each divorce/separation. That ratio would not be exceeded again until the 1850s. There was a steady progression in the number of separations throughout the period: from 1147 marriages per separation, to 110 in the last period before the change in law. In the period 1881–1886, there were but 83 marriages for every divorce. Table 4.11 details the growth in the absolute number of divorces, as well as the more refined rates of divorces per marriages. The growth in the number of divorces in France was less dramatic than that in the United States, yet there was a steady progression upward (save for a large number

Table 4.10.   Marriages, Divorces, and Separations in France, 1802–1886

Years	Marriages	Divorces/separations	Marriages to one div/sep
1802–1805	884,166	3,855	229
1806–1810	1,144,934	998	1,147
1811–1815	1,252,546	899	1,393
1816–1819	883,725	662	1,335
1820–1829[a]	241,091	273	883
1830–1839[a]	265,029	442	600
1837–1840	1,090,684	2,260	483
1841–1845	1,411,437	3,796	372
1846–1850	1,388,087	3,891	357
1851–1855	1,403,184	5,636	249
1856–1860	1,474,320	7,199	205
1861–1865	1,508,914	9,053	167
1866–1870	1,433,379	10,831	132
1871–1875	1,540,008	10,021	154
1876–1880	1,412,174	12,796	110
1881–1886	1,703,576	20,608	83

[a]The figures for 1820 to 1829 and 1830 to 1839 represent annual averages during those periods rather than the total number of marriages and divorces.
Source: U.S. Bureau of the Census. Special Reports. Marriage and Divorce 1867–1906, Part I.

reported, following World War I, in 1920) so that by 1930 there were four times the number of divorces reported as there had been in 1885. The divorces per 100 marriages had also climbed steadily, from 1.4 in 1885 to 6.8 in 1930.

Some details are known about the nature of divorces in the period 1887 to 1905 for France as a whole. We know that 35% of the divorces were sought by husbands, and 65% by wives. The cause most often cited was violence, cruelty, or dishonorable treatment, followed by the adultery of the wife and the adultery of the husband.[15] As in the United States, more than half of the divorcing couples had children during this period (56.3%), representing in excess of 125,000 dissolving families. The average length of time between marriage and divorce was estimated to be just under 10 years, and the average number of children per divorce was two.

More is known about divorces in Paris, which contributed a disproportionate share of divorces to the overall number reported for France (Special Census 1906). The modal age category of divorcing wives was 30–34 years, while the modal age category for husbands was 35–39 years. It is also known that more than 88% of both husbands and wives were single before their present marriage; 3.8% of the husbands and 3.6% of the

Table 4.11. Divorces in France, 1885–1930, 5 Year Intervals

Year	Total divorce	Divorces per 100 marriages	Divorces per 10,000 mar pop[a]
1885	4100	1.4	5
1890	6600	2.5	9
1895	7700	2.7	10
1900	7800	2.6	10
1905	10,900	3.6	13
1910	14,300	4.6	17
1915[b]	—	—	—
1920	34,800	5.6	41
1925	22,600	6.4	25
1930	23,400	6.8	24

[a] Persons divorcing per 10,000 married persons.
[b] Missing data. No official records available for France as a whole for the period 1915–1919.
Source: Adapted from Peter Flora, Franz Kraus, and Winfried Pfenning, *State, Economy, and Society in Western Europe 1815–1975*, Volume II, pp. 178–179.

wives were widowed, and less than 1% of these husbands and wives had been divorced previously.

As the custody of children in this period was decided predominantly on the basis of fault, we can gain some sense of the distribution of children from the award of divorce. In the period of 1887 to 1905 in Paris, it appears that 37.4% of the divorces were granted to husbands, 56.4% to wives, and 3.0% to both (3.2% were unknown).

Divorce in England

Pursuant to a Royal Commission on the Law of Divorce in 1850, in 1857 new legislation legalizing divorce was passed, making divorce available from the Court of Divorce (instead of the Parliament). The same ground remained as before: simple adultery for husbands and adultery aggravated by other causes for wives. These were insufficient reforms to generate a divorce rate comparable to other countries; nonetheless, the reduction in cost from hundreds (or thousands) of pounds to from 40 to 60 pounds (Phillips 1988) did serve to admit the upper middle classes to the ranks of the divorced (Savage 1983). Phillips (1988) notes another effect of the lowered cost of divorce, as well: this change in the law meant that the percentages of divorces sought by women changed from roughly 1% to 42% by 1909, (even though divorced mothers were almost certain to lose custody of their children during this time).

Table 4.12.   Divorces in England, 1860–1930, 10 Year Intervals

Year	Total divorces	Divorces per 100 marriages	Divorces per 10,000 mar pop[a]
1860	127	0.1	<1
1870	194	0.1	1
1880	340	0.2	1
1890	400	0.2	1
1900	494	0.2	1
1910	581	0.2	1
1920	3090	0.8	4
1930	3563	1.1	4

[a]Persons divorcing per 10,000 married persons.
Source: Adapted from Peter Flora, Franz Kraus, and Winfried Pfenning, *State, Economy and Society in Western Europe, 1815–1975,* Volume II, pp. 206–207, 1983.

In 1923 a modification of the divorce law was passed—against an outpouring of sentiment that equally passionate on both sides—that allowed simple adultery to be the sole grounds for divorce for both men and women. Since the only real departure from past practice was to make it easier for women to prove sufficient grounds for divorce, the number of petitions filed by women increased significantly, as was expected. For the first time in English history, women gained the dubious distinction of being more likely to seek divorce than men (Phillips 1988).

By comparative standards divorce rates for England are modest, although the rate of change is at least as striking as elsewhere, and perhaps even more so (see Table 4.12). There were but 127 divorces recorded in 1860; by 1920 that number had exceeded 3000. The divorce rate per 100 marriages is small throughout the late 1800s, remaining at 0.1 or 0.2 until 1920, when it jumps to 0.8.

The Class Character of Divorce

Unlike marriages, divorces were not equally distributed across class lines. Divorce began as an upper class phenomenon in England and France, and to a lesser extent in France, in large part because prior to the late 1800s, as noted earlier, the personal and monetary cost was prohibitive. The rich and powerful were prominent among the claimants and those interested in the turn of events surrounding various divorce laws. Glendon (1989) has suggested that Napoleon's interest in divorcing Josephine was at least in part responsible for maintaining the provision of divorce by mutual consent in the 1804 Civil Code.

Table 4.13. Class Distribution of Divorces in England

Occupation of husband	Divorces 1896–1906[a] (%)	In labor force 1901[b] (%)
Agriculture	2.4	7.3
Mining	1.5	5.3
Manufacture	21.2	32.1
Navigation and fishing	2.9	NA
Inland transport	3.7	NA
Trade	31.4	11.1
Domestic services	1.7	7.3
Professional	23.6	NA
Unspecified	11.6	NA

[a] *Source:* Special Census Reports, 1909.
[b] *Source:* Adapted from Peter Flora, Franz Kraus, and Winfried Pfennig, *State, Economy and Society in Western Europe, 1815–1975.* Volume II, p. 527, 1983.

In England, the most striking statistic is the one that reports that of all divorces in 1896–1906, 23.6% were granted to those in the professions (see Table 4.13). Although precise comparisons to the percentage in the labor force are unavailable, the percentage of males in the professions could not have been greater than 10%. The overrepresentation of professions is therefore notable. A disproportionate number of divorces were also granted to those in trade, which was on the high end of the occupational categories: they made up 31.4% of the divorces, but only 11.1% of the labor force. Those in manufacturing were underrepresented among divorces (21.2% of those divorced as against 32.1% in the labor force).

Comparable data across occupational categories are unavailable for France, unfortunately, although the occupational distribution of the husbands in divorce cases is known (see Table 4.14). There is a kind of bimodal distribution of divorces in France. Workmen and day laborers made up 37.4% of all divorces, proprietors, capitalists, and professionals made up 17.2%, well in excess of their representation in the labor force as a whole, and merchants and shopkeepers comprised another 20.3%. In combination, these two categories contributed more than 37% of the divorces for the period 1887 to 1904. We do know that whereas slightly more than 44% of those in the labor force were engaged in agricultural pursuits, farmers make up only 9.5% of the divorces.

The best information regarding the class distribution of divorce, however, comes from the United States. The divorce rates of occupational categories are quite detailed: we know, for instance, that glass workers made up 0.3% of all divorces, while iron and steel workers made up 0.9% of all divorces. This would be hard to interpret, however, without

Table 4.14.   Class Distribution of Divorces in France

Occupation of Husband	Divorces 1887–1904 (%)
Proprietors, capitalists, professionals	17.2
Merchants and shopkeepers	20.3
Farmers	9.5
Workmen, day laborers	37.4
Servants	5.3
No report	10.4

Source: Special Census Reports, 1909.

the excellent work of Preston and Haines (1991) on the 1900 census. Their income estimates allow comparisons by occupational category, and these can be seen together with the divorce rates for each category in Table 4.15.

The table is divided into those occupations that are overrepresented and those that are underrepresented among divorces. Among those overrepresented, the average annual income is $685, while among those underrepresented, the average annual income is $554. Were domestic and personal workers' salary removed from the calculations, the differences would be even greater. Nonetheless, aside from domestic and personal workers, the greatest overrepresentation of any occupational category in divorces is the professional/service category: it contributed 5.5% of the divorces, yet only 3.9% of the workers. Other occupational categories overrepresented are trade and transport workers, bakers, glass workers, printers, and, the royalty among workers, the plumbers (whose income, at $850 nearly equals that of the average income of professionals, $865). Occupational categories underrepresented are those in agriculture, miners, leather, textile and metal workers, food preparers, and iron and steel workers. Iron, steel, and metal workers, by virtue of their incomes, should exchange places in the table with domestic workers. Other than these exceptions, however, the overrepresented occupations in the divorce rate are generally those with the higher incomes.

Thus, in England, France, and the United States, there is an unevenness in the distribution of divorces across class: those in higher status occupations are overrepresented among the divorced. The implications of this for this study will be explored in detail, for this also meant that women and children affected by divorce were disproportionately from the middle and upper classes. Before considering these implications,

Table 4.15. Class Distribution of Divorces in the United States

Occupations overrepresented among divorces			Occupations underrepresented among divorces		
Occupation	%LF/%DIV [a]	$ [b]	Occupation	%LF/%DIV	$
Professional/ service	3.9/5.5	865	Agriculture	39.4/28.4	334
Domestic personal	13.0/24.0	332	Miners	2.1/1.8	482
Trade and transport workers	18.2/19.4	639	Leather	0.2/0.1	600
Bakers	0.3/0.4	629	Textile	0.9/0.3	530
Glass workers	0.2/0.3	740	Metal workers	0.6/0.3	665
Printers	0.5/0.6	743	Food preparation	0.3/0.2	607
Plumbers	0.3/0.4	850	Iron/steel workers	0.2/0.9	665
Average $		685			554

[a] Percent in the labor force, 1900/percent divorces, 1887–1906.
[b] Average annual income, 1900.
Sources: For Divorce Rates by Occupation: Special Census Reports, 1909. For percent in labor force and average income: Samuel Preston and Michael Haines, *Child Mortality,* Appendix 1, 1991.

however, it is necessary to ask whether the lower classes were, perhaps, seeking other avenues in marital dissolution, in particular, desertion.

Desertion: The Poor Man's Divorce?

Although the class character of formal divorce of the period under consideration is evident, some have suggested that perhaps desertion served the same purpose for the poor. The argument is that since divorce was prohibitively expensive for the poor, why not merely leave without benefit of divorce?

In considering desertion we must be mindful not to think of it in present terms. First, desertion without benefit of divorce would serve as a bar against remarriage of either partner. This would be a remarriage restriction for life, a price quite heavy for both parties to bear. The counterargument might be that a new marriage would be unnecessary; lovers might live without benefit of marriage. Here we encounter the folly of modern logic applied to the past.

It was more likely that there was informal desertion everywhere, and perhaps a disproportionate amount of desertion among Catholics, who were typically unable to obtain a divorce without renouncing their faith. Desertion was no doubt more feasible in the United States than elsewhere: there was a greater possibility of starting a new life without social stigma in another state,[16] and communities did not have the same abiding character that they did in England and France.

Yet permanent desertion is only one kind of desertion, and most likely it was the *less* common kind among the poor. More common was desertion prompted by economic desperation in which the deserter was in intermittent contact with his family, often sending money and returning from time to time (Monroe 1932; Colcord 1919). This was no less awful, but it was prompted by a different cause than marital unhappiness alone.

Finally, it is important to note that child custody was resolved by desertion in the same way as it was by death: the remaining parent had no competition. The welfare burden occasioned by desertion was of a different type than that occasioned by divorce; following desertion no private party (other than the mother) could be expected to assume the parental obligation. Married women who were deserted—and especially poor married women—were of interest to the state only if they could not find means of support. Whereas opportunities for women of the middle and upper classes in the labor market were nearly nonexistent, opportunities for poor women in poorly paid, nearly subsistence income jobs were plentiful. Here, though, we are getting ahead of the story. Questions of how women were to support themselves will be taken up in Chapter 7. What is relevant here is that the state's interest in women and men who were deserted—even if they had children—was limited to the cases in which they were unable to take care of themselves.

Conclusion

Despite national differences in the restrictiveness of legislation divorce rates were rising everywhere, and as a result ever greater numbers of children were subject to the custody determinations of the state. This put pressure on custody laws, which originally were intended in the event of death, and on judges who were increasingly called upon to decide between two fit parents.

To some extent, the state's interest in retaining the custody of children as a deterrent to divorce, and a punishment in the case of it, meant that, as more divorces were granted to women, men would more often lose custody of their children. But why in other cases? What impelled judges to decide in favor of mothers was not the failure of custodial fathers themselves, but other sources altogether.

In part, the state had worked its way into a conundrum. Custody had originally been tied to obligation: obligation of the father to provide protection, material support, and education. Yet with the increasing numbers of divorces and the increasing numbers of women who were gaining custody owing to their innocence in divorce cases decided by guilt, the basis by which children's welfare traditionally had been ensured was undermined. That this was not anticipated legislatively is interesting; judges were certainly facing these issues as the numbers of custody cases grew.

Yet there was another—and perhaps more pressing—problem. The class character of divorces is important for it left not only children, but women as well—relatively privileged women—with no basis of financial support. The state was certainly unwilling to take on the burden of providing for these women. The support of husbandless women already was a clear public issue by the 1880s (Abbott 1938b): state legislative debates about public relief for women—often revolving around the issue of mother's aid—reveal substantial concern about the problem, as do transcripts of arguments at the national level about the mission of the newly created United States Children's Bureau.

While the benefits of being able to end marriages detrimental to the well-being of the individuals involved—particularly women—have been well appreciated, the substantially greater welfare burden occasioned by these changes has been underappreciated.

In a sense, the problem of providing for divorced women was more serious than the problem of taking care of children because it was more long-term. Children could be expected to be self-supporting (either in the labor market or in marriage) by age 21 at the latest, but their mothers had no such prospects on the horizon. The problem was compounded because of their rapidly increasing life expectancy: among no other group was life expectancy increasing as greatly as among privileged white women.

Notes

1.   Japan provides an excellent counterexample to the argument that the cultural and historical traditions of seemingly less morally dissolute countries are responsible for their lower divorce rates. Japanese lawmakers learned the lesson that morals follow legal sanctions, at least in the case of marriage.

2.   Some countries provided assistance, at least in theory: in Germany, France, Holland, and Scotland, a poor person desiring a divorce—with a good

case *prima facie*—could obtain free legal assistance (Willcox 1891). I have been unable to gain any insight as to the use of these provisions.

3.   Christianity, Catholicism, and Judaism all have strictures against adultery. In none of them, however, is the suggested penalty divorce. That is a secular adaptation of the religious law.

4.   Alabama in 1923, Georgia in 1926, Maryland in 1929, Missouri in 1929, Mississippi in 1930, and Virginia in 1930.

5.   It may be the case that these figures underestimate the degree of actual adultery among wives; divorcing husbands and wives may well have made private agreements to name the husband at fault when the wife was really the adulterer. There are numerous reasons why this might have been the case. Where there were children, the parents may both have preferred that the children go to the wife, even though she committed adultery. Further, the stigma attached to the cuckolded husband outweighed that suffered by the betrayed wife. Prohibitions against remarriage of adulterers in many states also might have given impetus to deals about fault, especially when the husband preferred to see his wife remarried quickly, for financial reasons, perhaps.

6.   The missing percentages are the result of divorce cases for which this more detailed information is unknown. In the case of New York, 4.1% of the divorce cases do not contain this information.

7.   These states were Alabama, Arizona, Arkansas, Colorado, Florida, Georgia, Idaho, Indian Territories, Michigan, Mississippi, Montana, Nebraska, Nevada, New Hampshire, New Mexico, North Carolina, North Dakota, Oklahoma, Rhode Island, South Dakota, Tennessee, Texas, Utah, Vermont, Virginia, Washington, Wisconsin, and Wyoming.

8.   These states were Alabama, Arizona, Arkansas, California, Colorado, Delaware, Florida, Georgia, Idaho, Indian Territories, Indiana, Kansas, Kentucky, Michigan, Mississippi, Missouri, Montana, Nebraska, Nevada, New Mexico, North Carolina, North Dakota, Ohio, Oklahoma, Oregon, Pennsylvania, South Dakota, Tennessee, Texas, Utah, Virginia, Washington, Wisconsin, and Wyoming.

9.   It is only divorce and not marriage that is subject to this struggle.

10.   It was often sponsored or cosponsored by George W. Norris (Senator from Nebraska) who maintained that "Every time a home is broken up, the onward march of civilization is halted."

11.   Throughout the transcripts the welfare of children is hardly mentioned except in a very general fashion. If the cult of childhood was indeed changing, and children were the romanticized and valued objects that several researchers have suggested that they were becoming, that awareness had not translated itself into arguments for the public agenda.

12.   Known as Loi Naquet, after its author, M. Henri Naquet.

13.   The rejection was tested again in 1886 when a modification of the original law—for procedural reasons—became necessary. But the Senate this time was resolutely against the notion of automatic conversion to divorce, and when M. Henri Naquet made a plea for reconsideration, McIlwraith (1917) writes, "The Senate . . . with the bigotry of most converts, turned a deaf ear to the voice which had originally charmed it."

14.   Some desired to encourage remarriage quickly so that new unions might also produce children. This desire emanated from a concern with the falling birth rate, and ever-smaller population relative to that of its increasingly hostile neighbor, Germany. One notes again the unusual alignment of sentiments in the

late 1800s relative to the alignment of sentiments in our present debates: those who argued for liberalization of divorce laws were anxious to promote an increased birth rate.

15.   The percentages are 88.2% for violence, cruelty, or dishonorable treatment, 13.7% for adultery of wife, 8.2% for adultery of husband, and 2.5% for condemnation to infamous punishment (Special Census 1916). The numbers do not add to 100% as it was possible to cite more than one cause.

16.   Informal accounts of desertion made for good reading, and good speeches, especially around discussions of the Uniform Marriage and Divorce Act. The Minority Report of the House of Representatives, Committee on the Judiciary, filed by Representatives Ray, Taylor, Broderick, Buchanan, and Powers, told of this colorful case (1892, p. 3): "In a case recently arising in the State of New York, a man died in the State of Indiana, leaving a wife and children in New York, another wife in Indiana, another wife and children in California, and leaving real property in each of these States. Each wife took dower in the lands in the State of her residence. The New York wife was his lawful widow in New York State and his New York children were legitimate there. Here the decedent was first married, and here his first wife and family of children had always resided. The decedent had deserted this family many years before his death. No divorce had ever been pronounced by the New York courts, nor had this wife ever been made a party to any divorce proceedings by any process recognized by the courts of New York State, nor had this recreant husband ever sued for a divorce on any ground recognized as a cause of divorce by the laws of the State of New York. Himself a deserter from the family hearth, an eloper, he had charged his wife with desertion, and on that false charge, in another jurisdiction and without her knowledge, had obtained a divorce valid in California, and he had then married in that State and, after a time, repeated this performance, winding up his career in Indiana. Life was too short for him to make the circuit of the Union, but had he started earlier and shown a little more activity he might have done it without meeting any serious obstacle in the law."

Yet he got caught, in the end.

5

Longer Life But No Jobs:
The Dilemma for Women
following Divorce

The increasing divorce rate served as a powerful impetus in the reconsideration of paternal preference in custody, but it was not the only one.
The potential welfare burden occasioned by the increasing divorce rate
was exacerbated by the upward trend in increased life expectancy of
white women. The period of dependency of a nonworking divorced
woman would be considerably greater than the period of dependency of
any child. The influence of longer life on marriage has been noted, but
the influence of increased longevity on the lives of those who divorced,
particularly on the lives of divorced women, has not been discussed.
Although this had no necessary implications for the welfare of children,
it did have implications for state's interests. If middle-class women were
increasingly divorced women, who would provide for them? Maternal
preference in child custody offered one possible solution.

Women and men married in their twenties, and, on average, divorced
after 9 or 10 years of marriage. Although slightly higher than the mean
age at marriage in France and United States, the mean age at marriage in
England was remarkably stable for both males and females (Wrigley and
Schofield 1981): in 1851 the mean age at marriage was 26 for females and
27 for males, as it was in 1901. With an average length of marriage of 9 to
10 years, men and women typically would have been in their mid to late
thirties at the time of divorce. Were children involved they would have
been somewhere between birth and 10 years of age.

Life Expectancy for Women

How many years would a divorced woman—should she not
remarry—need economic support, either of her own or other's provi-

Table 5.1. England and Wales: Expectation of Life at Specific Ages: Females

Birth year	Age (years)							
	0	10	20	30	40	50	60	70
1838–1854	41.85	47.67	40.29	33.81	27.34	20.75	14.34	9.02
1871–1880	44.62	49.76	41.66	34.41	27.46	20.68	14.24	8.95
1881–1890	47.18	51.10	42.42	34.76	27.60	20.56	14.10	8.77
1891–1900	47.77	51.97	43.44	35.39	27.82	20.64	14.10	8.78
1901–1910	52.38	54.53	45.77	37.36	29.37	21.81	15.01	9.25
1910–1912	55.35	55.91	47.10	38.54	30.30	22.51	15.48	9.58

sion? This can be answered simply by asking how long she would be expected to live. Table 5.1 shows age-specific life expectancy rates in England and Wales. The table spans 80 years and shows a quite remarkable change in the expectation of life. At birth in the years 1838 to 1854, the expectation of life was 42 years, though if one lived through childhood, one could expect to live to one's sixties. Only 30 years later, 6 years had been added to the expectation of life at birth, and there was a steady increase upward in life expectancy at all ages. The effects of decreased infant and child mortality are evident by 1901: those born between 1901 and 1910 could expect to live to 52 years of age, and, after childhood, to over 65 years of age.

We can get a glimpse of some of these rates in the upper classes, as well, owing to Hollingsworth's (1957) study of the British Ducal families. The expectation of life for females born in the period 1830 to 1879 at age 5 was 60.1, and so exceeded the average rate by a fair degree. Five-year-old daughters of dukes born in the period 1880 to 1949 were blessed with a life expectancy of 68.6 years. Table 5.2 shows the expectation of life at ages 20, 40, and 60 for these upper class English females. Born in the period 1830–1879, at age 40 a woman could expect to reach her seventies. Thus, the expectation of life for the upper class anticipated the rates of the general population by about one generation.

The second portion of the table shows a comparison of the British ducal families with the European ruling families, and reports the expectation for females at ages 15 and 50 for women born between 1780 and 1879. These numbers lend further weight to the observation of the effects of class on the expectation of life, though the British families seem to be especially favored in longevity.

Although divorce was a greater probability for those in the upper portions of the class structure, it is unlikely that the very wealthiest were

Table 5.2. British Ducal Families: Expectation of Life: Females

Age	1830–1879	1880–1934
20	46.2	54.3
40	31.5	37.4
60	16.6	21.2

Age	British ducal	European ruling
15	49.6	45.6
50	24.2	21.0

Source: Adapted from T. H. Hollingsworth, "A Demographic Study of the British Ducal Families," 1957.

Table 5.3. France: Expectation of Life at Specific Ages: Females

Birth year	Age (years)							
	0	10	20	30	40	50	60	70
1817–1831	40.83	47.42	40.08	33.41	26.58	19.58	13.16	8.08
1861–1865[a]	40.55	48.75	41.60	35.10	NA[b]	NA	13.90	NA
1877–1881[a]	43.42	49.75	42.25	35.50	NA	21.42	14.58	8.83
1891–1900	48.72	51.53	43.59	36.44	29.10	21.64	14.58	8.72
1898–1903[c]	49.13	52.03	44.02	36.93	29.60	22.14	15.08	9.21
1908–1913	52.41	53.08	44.83	37.37	29.75	22.13	14.95	8.95

[a] Note gap between years between this and the following category.
[b] NA, not available.
[c] Note overlap with previous category.

among those most likely to divorce (Stone 1979). Thus, we would expect that the life expectancy of those women who were disproportionately at risk of divorce—those in the upper-middle and middle classes—would fall somewhere between that of the general population and the upper class.

Table 5.3 reports the rates of expectation of life at specific ages for women in France. Although they did not fare as well as their sisters in England overall, the trend was clearly in the same direction, and, in fact, the gains were greater for those at birth. Born between 1817 and 1865, at birth a female could expect to live to 41, and at age 20, to 60 years of age. By the later period, the improvement was considerable: born in the period 1908 to 1913, the expectation of life at birth was 52 years, and at age 20, it had grown to 65 years of age.

In the early period of the United States, only comparable statistics from Massachusetts are available. Born in 1850, life expectancy for females was 40, but born 40 years later, females could expect to live to 45. At age 20, the rates resemble more closely those in Europe: a birthdate of 1850 was marked by an expectation of life of 60 years and a birthdate of 1890, an expectation of life of 62 years; at age 40, the expectation was that females would live to 70 and 69, respectively. These data are reported in Table 5.4.

By 1900, statistics for the white population as a whole (as well as the nonwhite population) were available (also found in Table 5.4). At birth in 1900, the expectation of life was 51 years; by the period 1909–1911 this had grown already to 54 years.

Thus, in all three countries there was an upward trend in life expect- ↑ Life ancy for the female population.[1] The numbers reported can be consid- ered the minimum life expectancies for divorced women, since these *Expectancy*

Table 5.4.   Expectation of Life for Women at Specified Ages

Year	Birth	20	40	60
Massachusetts				
1850	40.5	40.2	27.9	17.0
1890	44.5	42.0	28.8	15.7
1900–1902	49.4	43.7	28.8	15.1
White Women, United States				
1900–1902	51.1	43.8	29.2	15.2
1909–1911	53.6	44.9	29.3	15.2
1919–1921	58.5	46.5	30.9	15.9

Source: Adapted from U.S. Census, Historical Abstracts, Vital Statistics, 1980.

women were drawn disproportionately from the higher classes, and would have disproportionately enjoyed these improvements. Yet were women living their lives as divorcees? Were there significant numbers of divorced women in each age group?

Age-Specific Marital Status in France and England

Fortunately, this question can be addressed, but only in France and England. Table 5.5 reports the numbers of divorced women in France by age, per 10,000 members of given age groups. Data are available for 1891, 1911, 1921, and 1931. The age category 45–54 is that with the greatest rate of divorced women reported for each year. This is true for age-specific married rates, as well; that is, the greatest number of married women reported for each year are also found in the age category 45–54. Yet there were significant numbers of divorced women in every age category starting with the category 35–44. This is the period that we would expect the greatest number of divorces to occur.

A detailed examination of one year—1911, for instance—reveals the pattern found for every year. In this year, 73 per 10,000 women aged 35–44 were divorcees. More had been added by the age 45–54: now, 104 per 10,000 were of divorced status, even though the married rate per age was not that significantly different. By 55–64 some of the attrition would have been due to death, and other, perhaps, to remarriage: the number of divorces in this age category is 87 per 10,000. The number of those married had also declined slightly. For the age category 65–69, 50 per 10,000 were divorcees; at ages 70–74, 15 retained a divorced status.

To get a sense of how women lived out their lives, however, Table 5.4 can be read on the diagonal. Of French women aged 35–44, 73 per 10,000 were divorcees. In 1921, some of them would be reported in the age category 45–54, which reported a divorced rate of 146, and, again we can follow them to 1931 in the age category 55–64, where, it is reported, 154 of 10,000 were divorced. This is, of course, a quite imperfect procedure: some will have died; some will have entered independently through divorce at later ages; some will have remarried; and it is impossible to partition with the available data. The point stands, nevertheless: some proportion of divorced women were living out their lives as divorcees.

There is one more insight to be gained from Table 5.4. Successive decennial years brought ever greater numbers of divorced women in each age category 45–54 and older, while the married rates for these same age categories either remained the same or declined. For instance, in the age category 55–64, the numbers of divorced women were 17 in 1891; by 1931, that number had grown to 154. In contrast, the married

Table 5.5. Numbers of Divorced and Married Women in France by Age per 10,000 of Respective Age Group, 1891–1931

Age	1891	1901	1911	1921	1931
20–24	— (467)	— (638)	2 (637)	1 (555)	1 (724)
25–34	6 (3703)	— (4102)	22 (4427)	50 (5785)	34 (487)
35–44	23 (6933)	— (7243)	73 (7472)	138 (7464)	110 (7615)
45–54	26 (7528)	— (7737)	104 (7811)	146 (7353)	165 (7591)
55–64	17 (7036)	— (7001)	87 (7045)	110 (6493)	154 (7591)
65–69	9 (5893)	— (5565)	50 (5534)	74 (4652)	78 (4106)
70–74	3 (3556)	— (2811)	15 (2751)	35 (2106)	63 (2919)
75+	2 (2327)	— (1452)	8 (1445)	NA	36 (1439)

Source: Adapted from Peter Flora, Franz Kraus, and Winfried Pfenning, State, Economy, and Society in Western Europe 1815–1975, Volume II, 1983.

rate was 7036 in 1891, but 7009 in 1931. No change had occurred in the age-specific married rate, though the age-specific divorced rate had grown by more than eight-fold. This same pattern occurred in the age category 45–54 (from 26 to 165), 65–69 (from 9 to 78), and 70–74 (from 3 to 63). The changes observed in the latter two age categories strengthen the argument advanced above: the greater life expectancy together with the increased divorce rate meant ever-greater numbers of women without the economic support afforded by marriage living for ever-longer periods of time.

Even though the data are far more limited for England—they are restricted to the years 1921 and 1931—the same kinds of observations can be offered (Table 5.6). In every age category but the youngest, the rate of divorcees increased from 1921 to 1931, while the marriage rate essentially remained unchanged. In some age categories this increase was dramatic: by twice or more in the age categories from ages 35 to 64. Further, some proportion of divorced women were certainly living the remainder of their lives as divorcees.

Why Not Remarry?

At the present time it is common for individuals to remarry following divorce, yet this cannot serve as our guide in contemplating remarriage following divorce around the turn of the century. In the period 1910–1914, the percentage of those who married, divorced, and remarried was just over 10% (Cherlin 1981).

To begin with, the restrictions were considerable. An adulteress found guilty was unable to marry her paramour, the one person who would be the logical remarriage partner *ever* in England, prompting the following editorial in the *London Times*:

> If no one else will, I should like to protest, not against the infliction of punishment upon the guilty, but against the infliction of a punishment that must plunge them still deeper in guilt. The repudiated adulteress is not to marry her paramour. What, then, is she to do? Driven from her husband's roof, driven from her father's, in many cases without the necessaries of life, though accustomed to all its luxuries, and, however reduced she may be, too ignorant, too helpless, and too infamous a creature to be able to earn her own living, what, I say, under these circumstances is she to do. . . . Will the slave of vice as soon as she is divorced become a spotless nun, a more than Griselda? Will she who has trampled on the most sacred laws submit to the mere *fiat* of empiricism? Certainly not; she will think it no sin to become the mistress of her paramour, since the law will not let her be his wife. . . . Recollect that when you forbid her to

Table 5.6. Numbers of Divorced (and Married) Women in England by Age per 10,000 of Respective Age Group, 18981–1931

Age (years)	1921	1931
20–24	2 (2700)	1 (2568)
25–34	8 (6342)	13 (6577)
35–44	9 (7427)	23 (7522)
45–54	7 (7211)	18 (7204)
55–64	5 (5997)	10 (6190)
65–69	4 (4412)	6 (4607)
70–74	3 (3252)	5 (3418)
75+	2 (1714)	3 (1752)

Source: Adapted from Peter Flora, Franz Kraus, and Winfried Pfenning, *State, Economy, and Society in Western Europe 1815–1975*, 1983.

marry her paramour you as good as forbid her to marry at all. . . . It is true that some one else besides her paramour may possibly marry the divorcee; but who—who but an utter profligate or an utter fool, who when his passion for her cools will ill-treat her, scorn her, and make her utterly miserable?. . . . Do not, then, punish her by plunging her headlong down a still deeper abyss. . . . She may only have slipped once. She may have much to offer in excuse. Let the horrible doom I have depicted be reserved for the worst class of adulteresses—those whose conduct has been so scandalous as to leave them no hope of remarrying. (reprinted in Milnes 1975, no date or pages given)

This letter not only describes the problem facing the adulteress, but also problems common to many divorcees: they were stigmatized by a failed marriage. Formal and informal sanctions worked in concert to discourage divorce, and, thereby, remarriage.

The list of restrictions on remarriage by state in the United States was considerable (see Table 5.7). These must be interpreted in light of the state's interests in providing incentives for husbands and wives to remain married, and in reserving the right of punishment of the guilty party in the case of divorce. In many states there was a waiting period of 6 months to 2 years. This often followed a period of separation, and the time necessary to obtain the divorce: a woman could be in marital limbo for 5 years or more.

Many states were explicit in their differentiation between guilty and innocent parties. In Illinois, for example, an adulterer of either sex had to wait 2 years to marry; others had to wait 1 year. In Louisiana, no doubt influenced by its French legal heritage, it was not possible for an adulterer to marry the person named as the paramour. The legal restrictions on remarriage in Mississippi stated that the court could stipulate that the guilty party would never be permitted to marry again. New York had the most complex prohibitions of all: the person guilty of adultery could not marry again as long as the other spouse was either alive or unmarried, or if the court modified the agreement and 5 years had passed and the conduct of the adulterer had been exemplary. North Dakota enacted a simpler version—no remarriage of the guilty party during the life of the innocent party. Tennessee modified that slightly— the guilty party cannot marry the person with whom she or he had committed adultery during the life of the innocent party—and Vermont instituted a 3 year waiting requirement for the same transgressions.

Finally, remarriage was made much more unlikely by the presence of children. First, there was the simple matter of relative desirability. Yet beyond this, under the law (as discussed in Chapter 2) new husbands were required to provide for the debts of their wives, which extended to include their children. While this obligation did not rule out remarriage altogether, it certainly must have had a dampening effect on the divorcees' prospects for remarriage.

Table 5.7.   Restrictions on Remarriage, by State 1870–1920

State	Restriction
Alabama	Court-directed as part of divorce decree
Georgia	Not during appeal of divorce
California	Waiting period of 1 year
Delaware	Guilty party cannot marry person with whom adultery was committed
District of Columbia	Guilty party in adultery cannot marry again (Code 1901)
Idaho	Six months waiting period
Illinois	Guilty party in adultery cannot marry for 2 years; others have to wait 1 year
Indiana	Two-year waiting period
Kansas	Six-month waiting period
Kentucky	Only one divorce allowed (for guilty party)
Louisiana	Wife has to wait 10 months; cannot marry person with whom adultery was committed
Maryland	Court may decree prohibition against guilty party marriage during lifetime of innocent party
Massachusetts	Guilty party has to wait 2 years
Michigan	Court decree, within maximum limit of 2 years of how long guilty party has to wait
Minnesota	(after 1901) Wait 6 months
Mississippi	Court can decree that guilty party not marry again
Nebraska	Wait 6 months

(*continued*)

Table 5.7. *(Continued)*

State	Restriction
New York	Complainant may marry again during lifetime of defendant, but a defendant adjudged guilty of adultery cannot marry again until the death of the complainant, unless the court modifies [due to remarriage of complainant][a], until 5 years have passed, and if conduct of defendant has been exemplary
North Carolina	After March 13, 1895, party guilty of abundant cannot marry during life of innocent spouse
	1889 Guilty husband cannot marry again during life of innocent wife
North Dakota	Code 1885—in adultery, guilty part cannot marry again during life of innocent party
	March 7, 1901: wait 3 months
Oklahoma	Wait 6 months; guilty party cannot marry during life of innocent
Oregon	Wait 6 months
Pennsylvania	Guilty adulterous party cannot marry person with whom one committed adultery
Rhode Island	Six months wait
South Dakota	Guilty party cannot marry during lifetime of innocent
Tennessee	Guilty party cannot marry person with whom one committed adultery during life of innocent party
Vermont	Guilty part cannot marry until 3 years, unless innocent party dies
Virginia	Court can decree that adulterer not marry again
Washington	(March, 1893) 6 months waiting
Wisconsin	May 1901: wait 1 year

No restriction: Arizona, Arkansas, Connecticut, Florida, Indian Territories, Iowa, Maine,[a] Maryland,[b] Missouri, Montana, Nevada, New Hampshire, New Jersey, New Mexico, Ohio, Texas, Utah, West Virginia, Wyoming

[a]Repealed an act February 17, 1887 wherein neither party could marry within 2 years after; guilty party could not marry without permission of court.
[b]Until 1888: Court may decree prohibition against marriage of guilty party during lifetime of innocent party.

Together, the low probability of remarriage and the increased life expectancy of women once again serve to emphasize the question: who was to take care of the divorced women, and especially those encumbered with children? One long-held notion is that these women would merely return to their families of origin.

Household Composition

Through the work of Mitterauer and Sieder (1982) and Laslett (1972), the myth of the norm of the extended family during this period has been dispelled. The average size of the nuclear family in Laslett's study of preindustrial communities is 3.8, with an average number of children of 2.1; and this is corroborated by Armstrong's (1972) study of the household structure of York in 1851, which found an average size of 3.5 per family, with about 1.8 children. In Hollingsworth's study (1957) of the British ducal families, the family size of the duke's daughters ranged from 2.5, among those married to commoners, to 3.9, among those married to peers. As Mitterauer and Sieder (1982, p. 40) remark, "It is not the nuclear family that is the result of industrialization and its accompanying modernization, but the increasing emergence of the incomplete family, in which there is no compulsion always to fill the two central roles."

The household composition of divorced and separated families in France in 1911 and 1936 is reported in Table 5.8. In 1911, nearly one-quarter had no children, nearly one-quarter had one, and one-fifth had two. Among those separated and divorced in 1936, again, nearly one-quarter had no children, more than one-quarter had one, and one-fifth had two.

Detailed information is available for household composition in Chicago, owing to a superb study based on unpublished Census materials (Day 1932). Of the 3220 broken families recorded in Chicago, 79.5% maintained their own homes, while 15.8% lived with relatives. There was a positive relationship between occupational status and likelihood of having a separate domicile. Figures are also available for women and men. Women were more likely to maintain a separate home (81.4%) than were men (71.4%), and women were less likely to live with relatives (14.9%) than were men (20.0%). Men were more likely to maintain a separate home when they had more children: 86% of those men with three children maintained a separate home, while only 58.1% of those with one child did so.

Household composition can also be described from the child's point of

Table 5.8.   Rate of Divorce/Separation by Number of Children, in France

Number of children	Per 1000 families	
	1911	1936
0	236	246
1	242	271
2	210	211
3	132	121
4	80	67
5+	100	84

Source: Adapted from *Statistiques Des Familles*, Service National des Statistiques, 1945.

Table 5.9. White Children's Living Arrangements in the United States, 1900[a]

	Total U.S. sample	
	N (total 1810)	%
One parent		
Male	573	31.66
Female	1229	67.90
Child in subfamily	(total 1397)	(4.72)
With no parent	538	38.51
With single parent	418	29.92
With both parents	244	17.47

	One parent household (%)	Mother-headed household		Father-headed household	
Location		N	%	N	%
Baltimore	9.4	8	100	0	0
Boston[b]	12.6	12	66.7	4	22.2
Washington D.C.	22.8	11	78.6	3	21.4
Kansas (rural)	9.7	30	58.8	21	41.2
Philadelphia	10.6	28	71.8	11	28.2
New York City	8.1	49	59.8	33	40.2

[a] These data were kindly provided by Sara McLanahan, and represent her work with Linda Gordon and Elaine McDonald.
[b] Missing data, does not add to 100%.

view. New research using a sample of 1900 Census materials (Gordon, McDonald, and McLanahan 1988)[2] classifies children by parental status (see Table 5.9). Of the 2228 children in the sample with one parent, 1810 of them, or 85%, were in a separate household (see Table 5.9). Of those 1810, two-thirds were with their mothers, and one-third were with their fathers.[3]

Although the numbers are extremely small, the distribution of one-parent households among fathers and mothers in various U.S. cities and one rural state prove interesting (see Table 5.9). New York City and rural Kansas are the two locales with the highest proportion of father-headed single-parent households (40.2 and 41.2%, respectively). This is no surprise in the case of New York, with its far more restrictive divorce and custody laws. Washington D.C. and Baltimore boast the highest proportion of mother-headed single-parent households.

These tables suggest that in most cases, it appears that women were heading their own households, and the Chicago families study suggests that women were more likely to do so than men, even when men cared for their children. The problem of the support of women following divorce was not solved by a large-scale exodus back to the family of origin. Thus we are still without an answer to the question of who was to take care of the divorced women and their children. Some might suspect that perhaps it was the women themselves who provided for their own support.

Disadvantage of Women in the Labor Market

There were four sources of disadvantage to divorced mothers in the labor market: first, they were women, second, they had been formerly married, third, they were divorced, and fourth, they had children. Each served as a separate impediment to self-support; together they rendered women nearly economically powerless to provide for themselves and their children.

Among all white women in the United States in 1900, 16.3% were in the labor force. The handicap associated with gender was expressed clearly in the ratio of earnings within occupations. Goldin's study (1990) permits us to say just how much of a gender gap existed in 1890/1900. Those working in sales suffered least: their earnings were 60% of those of males. Women working in manufacture, service, and agriculture earned roughly 53% of their male counterparts. Yet, it was in the higher status occupations that the gap was the greatest: clerical workers earned just under half of what male clerical workers earned but professional women earned just 26% of what male professionals earned. These were the earnings of the fully employed. Part-time work cannot have been more adequately compensated.

Furthermore, occupations were typically sex-segregated, particularly in manufacturing:[4] women were concentrated among textile workers and apparel workers. Within-occupational differences are telling. Goldin (1990, p. 76) reports in detail on the case of compositors:

> Compositors around 1900 typeset handwritten copy often continuing numerous idiosyncratic abbreviations; they were skilled workers, often well educated. The occupation was integrated in the 1860's after the union received assurances that women would be brought in at "scale" . . . Only 12 [of 41] firms were integrated by sex, where integration means having at least one male and one female compositor. Most women were paid by piece and worked in integrated firms; most men were paid by time and worked in nonintegrated firms. Piece-rate payment dominated for both in the integrated firms. Within the integrated firms, men were paid about 35% more than women, although piece rates were identical.

Women in England were also barred from numerous occupations in the professions, as well as in lower status jobs. Medical professions, for instance, prevented women from entering by restricting their admission to the necessary training (Atkins and Hoggett 1984). The origins of sex segregation undoubtedly began in school, where the curriculum after 1870 was controlled centrally, and financial awards were given to schools that established domestic curricula for girls, thereby effectively narrowing their occupational opportunities (Atkins and Hoggett 1984).

Whatever the cause of the lower rates of pay, however, the importance for the case at hand is simply that women would be unlikely to be able to support themselves, or their children. If the further caveat is added that they should be able to support themselves in the manner to which they were accustomed when married, this would have been impossible.

Married and Divorced Women in the Labor Force

The practice of marriage bars—formal and informal restrictions on married women's participation in the labor force—have been nearly forgotten. Atkins and Hoggett (1984) report the history of the development of such prohibitions on married women's labor in England, beginning in the 1840s. Women (and children) were formally barred from underground mining by the Mines and Coleries Act of 1842, and women's work in factories was regulated by the Factory Act of 1844. They note that the motivations were not merely protective:

> As the Report of the Commissioners on Mines and the parliamentary debates on both the Mines and Factory Acts show, it was not the gruelling hard work which outraged Victorian society but the immorality of women engaged in such work. In the case of young women horror was expressed at the close proximity of men and women in both mines and factories. . . . Perhaps even more concern was expressed at the greater immorality of married women who, it was alleged, left their homes and families, neglected their domestic duties and forced their menfolk to seek the comforts of public houses, thus subjecting the next generation to 'all the evils of a disorderly and ill-regulated family.'(Atkins and Hoggett 1984, pp. 12–13)

The factory legislation formally excluded women not only from mining but from working on moving railway cars, from maintaining and working moving machinery, and, more generally, from night work. Restrictions on hours naturally lowered pay.

The specific limitations on married women exceeded those even on women in general. Public service jobs were unavailable to women through the operation of the marriage bar until World War II (Atkins and

Hoggett 1984). Further, the seemingly progressive Sex Disqualification (Removal) Act of 1919, requiring professions to lift restrictions against women, left the marriage bar intact:

> Despite its broad wording the courts held that the introduction of a marriage bar did not contravene the Act's provisions; nor had any individual who was refused a job any right of litigation under it. The Act merely required the professions to lift their restrictions against women. A particular employer was still at liberty to restrict a particular job to one sex or to unmarried workers. In *Price v. Rhondda Urban Council* [1923] 2 Ch. 372, Mr. Justive Eve rejected the argument that a marriage bar was in restraint of marriage and therefore contrary to public policy: 'It would in any opinion be pressing public policy to intolerable lengths to hold that it was outraged by this Authority expressing a preference for unmarried women over married women.' (Atkins and Hoggett 1984, p. 17)

Marriage bars operated, as well, in the United States, and followed similar patterns to those noted in England. However, specific marriage bars arose in the most important employment available to middle-class women: in teaching, beginning in the late 1800s, and in clerical work (Goldin 1990). The marriage bar had its effect: 10% of all married women worked in England. In the United States, 2.5% of the labor force was made up of married women.

It is not clear what percentage of divorced women worked, though figures are available for the combined category of divorced and widowed women (Goldin 1990). In 1890 that figure was over 40% for women 25–44, and just over 30% for those in the 45–54 age category (Goldin 1990, p. 18). Just 15.5% of those, however, were white (Goldin 1990, p. 26). By itself, divorce was a sufficient stigma to prevent women from finding appropriate jobs: divorced women were largely excluded from the middle-class occupations of teaching and nursing in the United States and England. Yet the marriage bar also had an extended effect: that it kept many women from working during marriage meant that they would have been entering the labor force following a period of 9 to 10 years without relevant job experience. Add to that the handicaps of middle-age and dependent children and a bleak employment picture results.

Who Would Care for the Women and Children following Divorce?

The convergence of demographic pressures together with significant, entrenched labor market discrimination aimed particularly at the very women who were disproportionately subject to the risk of divorce made

the question of the economic welfare of women following divorce particularly critical. Nearly all avenues of support were denied to divorced
mothers. There were, however, two remaining possibilities: the state
and the fathers of their children.

Notes

1.   A less dramatic but still positive trend in expectation of life is observed for
males, as well, in all three countries.
2.   Kindly provided to me by Sara McLanahan.
3.   What proportion of these single-parent households owed their origin to
divorce or separation—as against death, illegitimate birth, desertion, or any
other circumstance—is not known. It is likely, however, that given the relatively
young ages of the parents, divorce was more likely than death to be the cause.
4.   Goldin (1990, Chapter 3) estimates the index of dissimilarity in the manufacturing sector to be around 91.

6

Financial Obligations to Fathers, Education to the State: Parcelling the Needs of Children

The lives of women, especially middle- and upper-middle class white women, were elongated at the same time as those same women were being increasingly subject to the risk of divorce, and excluded from suitable occupations. Although a longer life and increasing possibilities of release from undesirable marriages might have prompted a greater sense of well-being, these positive sentiments were tempered by the curtailment of their liberties as independent actors by virtue of the realities of restrictions in occupational and income opportunities. A woman's freedom from marriage did not resolve the problem of her dependence, no less so if she won the custody of her children. Focusing on the freedoms won by women to divorce and to keep their children diverts attention from the yoke of financial provision following marriage. To whom that yoke would be attached was an all-important question as the divorce rate continued to rise.

As privileged divorced mothers were poor candidates to provide for themselves, in large part because of the considerable discrimination exercised against them in the labor force, there were but two parties left: the state and fathers. This chapter will examine the unwillingness of states to assume that welfare burden generally. In the process, it will become clear that children, and, to a lesser extent, wives and ex-wives, were, in the general scheme of things, to be considered private obligations rather than public concerns. Yet the sense of the period—in the United States, though not so much in France or England—is one in which the welfare obligations toward children and mothers were growing, as captured in the growth of maternalist social policies (Skocpol, 1992). How are these two—the privatization of familial financial obligation on the one hand and the growth of social welfare policies aimed at women and children in the United States on the other—to be reconciled?

Maternalist Social Policies in the United States[1]

By 1930, all but four states[2] had enacted social policies designed to redress the economic plight of widows and their children. It would seem a small step to extend this to divorced women and their children, but this would not, in fact, be done. The reasons why such a step was never taken can be found in the account offered for the unusual success of maternalist social policies in a climate antithetical to the extension of social welfare more generally.

Skocpol (1992) offers several reasons for their success. The first was that the argument for mothers' pensions was one that was consistent with the general ideological tenor of the period: children should be kept with their mothers.[3] The fate of the children of the women who would be affected by such legislation was tenuous, at best: were they not to stay with their mothers—who were often working—they were likely to end up in institutions. Despite the seemingly unimpeachable logic, both on grounds of emotion and public finance, there was some controversy.

The objections to this promaternalist logic were lodged primarily by private reformers. These individuals—predominantly women—had a vested interest in protecting their own private charitable work, which largely centered on remedying the various plights of poor children. One of the tacks taken in their opposition was that past public expenditures in a similar vein—namely, Civil War pensions—had created an unwieldy and ever-greater public burden. Why give rise to a similar problem, they argued, when the history of the past one is known, and is insupportable?

Yet their voices were overcome by the cooperative and organized efforts of professional reformers and various associations of married women, not the least important of which was the National Congress of Mothers. Their case rested on two, related grounds. The first was the recognition of the importance of motherhood: the care that a mother could give her child was superior to any other, and especially to any provided by an institution, private or public. (These were the same sort of arguments as those that were a part of the so-called cult of motherhood. See Chapter 3.) Although their arguments were intended to apply to unfortunate, widowed mothers, the women who were advancing them—largely well-educated middle class women—were no doubt affirming their own motherhood, as well.[4] The other support for this sort of argument came from the shift from an emphasis on children's rights to those of women and mothers.'

The last impetus to which these maternalist policies owed their success was the explicit and implied emphasis on family stability. In 1911, the National Congress of Mothers enunciated the following (quoted in Skocpol 1992, Chapter 7):

> *Resolved.* That it is the sense of this Congress that families should, if possible, be held together. That the mother is the best caretaker for her children. That when necessary to prevent the breaking up of the home the State should provide a certain sum for the support of the children instead of taking them from her and placing them elsewhere at the expense of the State.

The proposal thus contained within it the suggestion that the state would end up paying either way; this was to some extent its very rationale.

But states were not without alternatives in the case for divorced mothers: the state did not need to pay either way; there was a private party who could be obligated to pay, instead of the state. In fact, each cause of the success of maternalist social policies, with the exception of the emphasis on true motherhood, is simultaneously a reason why no state support would be forthcoming for divorced women. *That there was no private party available as an alternative to the state in the case of widowed and deserted mothers was the basis for the strength of their claims.* Furthermore, the reliance on the notion of the stability of the family—together with the opposition to divorce of many of the women who were members of the National Congress of Women and other domestically conservative women's groups—excluded divorced women from consideration.[5] The shift in emphasis from children's rights to women's rights was also damaging: to make the case for mothers' pensions for divorced women, it would be necessary to argue that children's welfare would be enhanced, either because they were materially better off or because they were advantaged by being with their mothers. Yet these claims could not be reasonably advanced as long as fathers were available to take the custody of their children.[6] Finally, the focus in this legislation was primarily on poor women and children, yet a disproportionate number of divorced women and children were of the same classes as those who battled for these reforms. The fathers of those children could be expected to have ample resources to shoulder the financial burdens of their children and ex-wives.

Another difference—a theoretical one—differentiated divorced and widowed women in their claim to state support. There is a moral hazard problem (Heimer 1985) associated with divorce that is not characteristic of widowhood. Widowhood is a state that is not under the control of the wife. A certain number of men get killed in war, and widowhood results. As such, widowhood is a status that is a risk for any woman whose husband fights in a war.

Divorce, however, is a state that is under the actor's control, to some extent at least. At this period of time it was thought to be associated with moral failure. Taxpayers could not expect to be interested in subsizing moral corruption, especially when the parties might have brought it upon themselves.

Unwillingness to Fund Paternalist Policies

There were many alternatives never discussed to relieve the financial plight of widows. One suggestion never made was that the state ensure that the salaries paid to widows for their work be equivalent to those paid to men for theirs. The adoption of mothers' pensions contained an implicit recognition and tacit support of the existing gender gap in income. Further, why should widowed fathers not be similarly eligible for pensions? Even a poor father was certainly preferable to an institution, just as a poor mother was. This was never considered, of course: just as women were to mother, men were to provide.

Nearly all of the rather limited social welfare available in the nineteenth century was of a private sort: in France, it was entirely private (Saint-Jours 1982). The Catholic church, various Friendly Societies, employers, and private insurance schemes were the extent of what was available beyond the family. Employers' social welfare schemes anticipated, by several decades, those of the state. Family allowances—designed to dampen competition between single and married workers and to obviate the need for general wage increases—were available on a limited basis from employers. Welfare of children was established as a separate enterprise in 1904, for children of the poor, and neglected children for whom the state would assume guardianship.

The famous Poor Laws of England were predicated on the link between welfare and work: paupers were confined to workhouses. Even the modification of poor law relief, allowing relief outside the workhouse in exceptional cases, was tied to specified work obligations (Ogus 1982). Unlike in the United States, relief for widows was unavailable. Insurance companies thwarted an early attempt in 1911 to include widows' pensions in a national insurance scheme, though in 1925, this was amended in favor of widows' pensions, regardless of age, but dependent on future marital status. As in the United States, there was no extension to divorced women. Ogus (1982, p. 197) notes: "The single-parent, condition . . . was not a risk which a social insurance scheme could embrace: administratively (and *sub silentio* politically) it was not feasible, particularly as it would involve some investigation into the cause of the breakdown."

Reiteration of the Father's Private Obligation

The maternalist policies and child welfare provisions that characterized this era did not extend to divorced wives and children of broken marriages. Fathers separated from their children through divorce were not to be separated from the financial obligation for them or for the mothers of those children; fathers continued to be held responsible. This difference rendered divorced women fundamentally unlike widows and their children in the eyes of the state, and in the eyes of the public, as well. State's interests were served by reiterating fathers' private obligations to provide material support.

Whereas noncustodial fathers maintained their financial obligation to their children and the mothers of their children after divorce, custodial fathers continued to provide only for their children.[7] *From a social welfare point of view, this made the arrangement whereby fathers were noncustodial parents a superior arrangement,* for it provided for not one set of dependents, but two.[8] Thus these states had a clear economic imperative to prefer maternal presumption of custody over paternal presumption of custody: it forestalled what could otherwise become a severe public burden, namely welfare provision for divorced women.

Thus material support for children would remain with fathers whether or not the children themselves did, for it was in the states' interests on three dimensions: first, it privatized the obligation, second, it solved, at least during the period of children's dependency, the problem of support of divorced mothers, and third, it avoided a public debate on the issue of discrimination against women in the labor force that certainly would have been necessary had divorced women been expected to provide for themselves and their children.

The decision to privatize the material support of children (and women) following divorce left one obligation: the obligation to educate. Formerly a major part of the father's responsibility, states everywhere were assuming this burden. Although education is a welfare burden, states assumed the obligation, not to relieve fathers, but rather for their own ends.

Transferring Education to the State

Referring to the United States, Puxon (1971, p. 168) wrote: "In 1893 school attendance was made compulsory: the father's moral duty to educate his children was converted into a legal duty, and at the same time the state took the obligation to provide schooling off his shoulders." The effect would be to remove the last remaining barrier to the presumption of maternal custody.

Remarkable changes in public education in this period are evident in all three countries. Table 6.1 describes these changes in the United States. Although described nationally, the control of schools was a local and privately funded affair. Schools often were tied to churches (until 1833), supervised by parents, and paid for through fees and endowments (de Swaan 1988). Across the country, changes in the nature and extent of schooling were far from uniform: Connecticut was first in providing education to factory children (1813); Massachusetts compelled the support of schools through taxation (1827); Pennsylvania made the public provision of education general rather than confining it simply to the children of the indigent (1834); and Massachusetts adopted the first compulsory school attendance law (1836), followed soon thereafter by Rhode Island (1840) and Connecticut (1842) (Bremner 1971). Funding was always an issue, and it often became a matter of contest between religious denominations: Protestants and Catholics tangled over issues of school control and funding, as did Protestants and Quakers (de Swaan 1988). Cities, confronted with increasing diversity in their populations and strong ethnic organizations, juvenile delinquency, and complex politics, opted for expanded, professionally run schools to address some of these issues. In the South, there were problems of entirely a different sort. The persistent segregation of blacks, together with the efforts of the North to break the Southern elite's hold on local educational systems, created a Northern-based philanthropic movement oriented toward public education found in no other region.

Despite these considerable variations, however, the trend toward increasingly public, secular, and compulsory education was unstoppable, and is represented by the figures in Table 6.1. The number of pupils enrolled in school from 1870 to 1920 increased by a factor of three (while the population of children increased by two). Whereas in 1870 only 57% of children aged 5–17 were enrolled in school, by 1920, 77.8% were. Even the average number of days of attendance per pupil rose two-fold.

Public financial commitments increased apace. Revenue collected for disbursement to schools jumped from 143 million to 970 million in this period from 1870 to 1920. The total expenditure per capita of population rose from $1.64 to $9.80; total expenditure per pupil began at $15.55 and ended in 1920 at $64.16. The education that had once been reserved for those who could pay privately was now extended to many more who could not have afforded the cost of their children's education.

Not surprisingly, although the English and French patterns of attendance and state provision showed roughly the same trend, there were some differences. In France universal elementary education with compulsory attendance was established through the Loi Guizot of 1833 (de Swaan 1988). Religious tugs-of-war that had always been a feature of

Table 6.1.   Statistical Summary of Changes in Schooling in the United States

	1870	1890	1910	1920
Pupils enrolled	6,871,522	12,722,631	17,813,852	21,578,316
Children 5–17 enrolled (%)	57.0	68.61	73.49	77.80
Average number days attended	78.4	86.3	113	121.2
Expenditure per capita population	$1.64	$2.24	$4.64	$9.80
Expenditure per pupil	$15.55	$17.23	$33.23	$64.16

Source: Adapted from U.S. Bureau of the Census, Historical Abstracts, 1980.

conflict over schools in France were addressed in this law: parents could choose between public and private schools. Yet though this seemed reasonable, it only gave rise to new kinds of conflict (de Swaan 1988, pp. 96–97):

> The Loi Guizot was only the beginning of very many new conflicts, this time at the village level. The local notables feared that the literate peasants would not need their services anymore and that the educated youngsters would prefer the city to the village. The nobility and the clergy did what they could through endowments, intrigue and slander to frustrate the efforts of the public schoolteacher. And the antagonism was mutual, the mayor siding with the public schoolteacher who often doubled as his secretary. Both sides tried to pack the school board and the communal council . . . once Louis Napoleon came to power the tables were turned again in favor of the church with the Loi Falloux (1850), a law adopted 'to moralise education too cut off from religion'. The difficult life of the school teacher became miserable. 'Isolated in his village, subject to the pressures of local notables, cut off by salary from the middle class and by education from the peasantry, the *instituteur* was prey to retaliatory persecution, encouraged by successive government measures.'

The politics of schooling was always a rich affair, hardly tainted by a spoken word of concern for children's education!

Class differences played a role, too, for financing was a matter for local authorities. Thus the difference between working class and bourgeois schools widened, all financed publicly. Yet, by 1882, a law had been introduced instituting 7 years of mandatory education. The law had its intended effect (see Table 6.2): by 1906, 85.1% of those in the age

Table 6.2.   School Enrollment in France, 1850–1906

Year	Aged 5–14 enrolled (%)
1850	51.5
1863	66.5
1866	69.1
1876	73.6
1886	82.0
1896	83.3
1906	85.1

Source: Adapted from Peter Flora, Franz Kraus, and Winfried Pfenning, *State Economy and Society in Western Europe 1815–1975*, Volume I, 1983.

category 5–14 were enrolled in school, up from 51.5% in 1850, and 73.6% in 1876.

The relative decline of children in private schools is also noteworthy, for it gives support to the claim that those who had formerly paid for their children's education were now taking advantage of the state's largesse. Over a third of children in schools in 1863 were enrolled in private schools (37.1%). This proportion had declined to 27.2% by the turn of the century, and fell to 18.9% by 1930 (Flora et al. 1983).

Finally, in England, as in France, the conflict over control of education was dominated by issues of religion, this time, prompted by the over-weening control of the Anglican Church. Though the Anglicans exercised a strangle-hold over local education, Anglicans and dissenters struggled for access to and control of state funds for education (de Swaan 1988).

Class struggles were superimposed upon religious ones. Interestingly, those among the labor aristocracy often preferred private, non-Anglican education for their children, and were willing to pay for it (de Swaan 1988). Together with their press for better working conditions, and against child labor, they could find no common ground with the bour-geoisie who were interested in the continuing cheap labor of children.

In time some of these matters would be resolved through the Elementary Education Act of 1870, that served to structure local educational institutions. This was followed by compulsory attendance laws in 1880, which insisted on 8 years of education for each child, and free elementary education in 1893. The consequences are apparent in Table 6.3. Only 10% of children aged 5–14 were in school in 1855; by 1885 this number had grown to more than half, and by 1914, to 79%.

Schooling had irretrievably become the province of the state by the turn of the century. Despite differences in systems of governance, de-spite differences in religions, despite differences in sizes of population,

Table 6.3. School Enrollment in England, 1855–1914

Year	Aged 5–14 enrolled (%)
1855	10.6
1865	19.1
1875	34.1
1885	54.1
1895	70.9
1905	78.0
1914	79.0

Source: Adapted from Peter Flora, Franz Kraus, and Winfried Pfenning, *State Economy and Society in Western Europe 1815–1975*, Volume I, 1983.

in each of these three countries, the power and the obligation to educate had been transferred from fathers to the state.

Unintended Consequences

Neither the privatization of postdivorce welfare of women and children nor the public control of education was intentionally designed to bring about a change in the presumption of child custody following divorce. Nevertheless, each had a powerful effect. In the first case, the ideological line separating women and children left dependent by the death of the male breadwinner from women and children left dependent by the voluntary breakup of marriage was clearly demarcated. When men were available, they would be called upon to provide. The argument for maternal custody was never mounted publicly on these grounds. Far more gentle appeals, based on children's needs for mothers' nurture, were instead the stuff of public discourse. However, given that equally compelling ideological statements on behalf of paternal custody were made only a few decades earlier, the logic of change seems to reside instead in the legislators' own interests as well as the general economic interests of the state. Those who doubt that the state's economic interests are compelling in the matter of policy with respect to children should consider the substantial state resources devoted to compelling fathers of children on welfare to pay child support, but comparatively less to compelling fathers of other children to pay (Garfinkel and McLanahan 1986). The benefits to children are arguably greater in the latter case, yet the savings to the state are greater in the former case.

In the second case, states—for reasons entirely separate from concerns about the welfare of children following divorce (and perhaps also separate from concerns about the welfare of children at all)—took on the "moral heart" of the father's obligation toward his children by providing public education.

The exclusion of divorced women from maternalist social policies had the unintended effect of encouraging maternal presumption in child custody disputes. So too did the advent of compulsory free public schooling. The first had this effect because vesting custody with mothers ensured support for both children and mothers whereas vesting custody with fathers solved the problem of postdivorce financial support only for children. From the state's point of view, this was a clearly superior solution. The second had this effect because it removed the last impediment to the award of custody to mothers. Mothers could provide nurture as well if not better than fathers could, but they were unable to provide for costly schooling, just as they were unable to ensure adequate material support for their children. Each trend in this period rich in social transformation would have profound implications for children's subsequent well-being.

Notes

1.   The discussion of maternalist social policies is based almost entirely on Skocpol (1992).
2.   The states without Mothers' Pension in 1930 included Alabama, Georgia, New Mexico, and South Carolina.
3.   One might think of this as the reiteration of the principle of privatization of the care of children.
4.   This argument is quite reminiscent of that advanced in Luker's (1984) book on the abortion movement, in which she suggests that the women who adopted a strong antiabortion stand were in part prompted to do so to enunciate the justifications for their own life choices.
5.   The domestically more radical single professional women had, as discussed in Chapter 3, split on the issue of custody of children entirely. As it was antithetical to their interests in getting ever-greater numbers of women in the labor market, some of them were not at all sure that children should not, in fact, be awarded to their fathers.
6.   Perhaps it is necessary to offer a reminder here that the impetus for the change in custody law did not come from a failure of paternal custody—that is, the change does not owe its origin to fathers' unwillingness to take custody of their children, and then care for them.
7.   Alimony provisions were rare. In the United States, no more than 30% of divorced wives received alimony until the 1950s, and in all three countries, alimony was a possibility almost exclusively in the case of the wife's innocence in divorce.
8.   I am using the term social welfare in the traditional sense: an arrangement that makes a greater number of people better off is superior to an arrangement that makes a fewer number of people better off.

7

The Structure of Indifference

In the face of increasing rates of divorce, changes in laws and demography, and shifting preferences, the fundamental needs of children remain constant. Children are highly dependent on the family for their welfare, and states depend on families to contribute to social order by raising productive citizens.

Divorce need not pose risks to children or societies, but it does in a system of social organization in which the stability of families, from the point of view of the child, depends on the persistence of marriage.

The history of custody tells us that the reason for vesting custody with fathers was that they had the sole responsibility for financially supporting, educating, and protecting their children. The separation of custody and responsibility occurred during the transition from paternal to maternal custody. This began when the state—for reasons quite separate from any concern over children of divorce—took over the educative function, thereby removing one of the three cornerstones of the father's responsibility. This was, in Locke's imagination, akin to snatching away the moral heart of the father's obligation to his children. Further, physically separating fathers from their children removed the second cornerstone of paternal obligation: protection. Financial responsibility—the most impersonal of the three—was all that remained. *Finance only remains*

At the advent of the preference for mothers over fathers in matters of custody, mothers were responsible to their children for nurture, fathers for financial support, and the state for education. Responsibility was diffused among the three.

Further, it is not just that there is no single responsible party, it is that the responsibility for children is spread among three agents who may be presumed to have quite different interests. Custody arrangements pretend that this is not so. When custody is awarded to one parent or another, that parent is then declared the agent of the child. But it is not an idle observation that the custodial parent's interests may not only diverge from her child's interests, but also from the father's and the state's with respect to the child.

119

The structural outcome of the historical changes in custody law is marked by a diffusion of responsibility, the properties of which are clearly documented in social–psychological literature. Diffusion of responsibility is one of three social–psychological processes that explain social inhibition or "bystander apathy" in the presence of others (Latane, Nida, and Wilson 1981; Latane and Nida 1981, p. 309).[1] The importance in the case of investment in children is that the mere presence of others who might intervene on the child's behalf constrains each of the actors involved. The presence of others reduces the psychological cost associated with nonintervention: "When others are present, such costs are shared and nonintervention becomes more likely. The knowledge that others are present and available to respond, even if the individual cannot see or be seen by them, allows the shifting of some of the responsibility for help to them" (Latane and Nida 1981, p. 309).[2]

Whereas a division of labor with respect to the child is likely in intact families, and each person's contribution under the scrutiny of the other, diffusion of responsibility is the corollary process in a divorced family. The ambiguity of the definition of the child's best interest further contributes to the probability of nonintervention. It is sufficient that each believe—but not observe—that others will help (Latane and Nida 1981). As responsibility is diffused, so is potential blame.

What is then interpreted as moral or altruistic action of parents toward children in intact families may owe more to the structure of those families than to the internal impulses of parents. Reflecting on the behavior of their subjects who failed to intervene when others were present, Latane and Darley (1969, p. 260) noted, "However much we wish to think that an individual's moral behavior is divorced from considerations of personal punishment or reward, there is both theory and evidence to the contrary. It is perfectly reasonable to assume that, under circumstances of group responsibility for a punishable act, the punishment or blame that accrues to any one individual is often slight or nonexistent."

The transition from the preference for fathers to the preference for mothers thus had an unintended consequence for children: the creation of a structure in which no one takes primary responsibility for the child of divorce. Indeed, instead of the historical record revealing each parent seeking to provide more resources and better care for their children, it reveals a game of hot potato played by mothers, fathers, and the state in which each wants the other to bear the costs of the children. It is not that mothers and fathers do not want custody of their children; newspapers and magazines are full of heart-wrenching custody battles. It is that their interests are served best when they gain custody—preferably sole custody—while others bear a substantial portion of the costs.

The transformation in institutions governing custody did not come about because of a radical revision of what was seen to be in the best interests of the child. The case was never made that fathers were unable to serve their children's interests. Fathers of the nineteenth century did not receive custody of their children as their just desserts and then suddenly cease to become deserving. If many fathers have become unable or unwilling to fulfill their paternal obligations, it is a consequence of the change in structure rather than an impetus for it. Similarly, mothers were not undeserving of the custody of their children prior to the turn of the century, only then to suddenly become deserving.

Instead, maternal preference in custody was an ingenious answer to several problems simultaneously. First, maternal custody served to increase the probability of private party support for two dependents rather than only one. The logic that had given weight to fathers in intact families could be extended to divorced ones: fathers were obligated to their children for support. This obligation was measurable and enforceable, and so did not depend on fathers' interest alone. By paying for the room and board of the children, fathers indirectly paid for room and board for mothers. Paying alimony—when it was awarded—was a way of paying for child care.

Second, maternal custody put off questions concerning the problematic access of middle-class women to the labor market. If they were not to be obligated to support themselves and their children, they would have a much weaker claim to equal pay and expanded opportunities.

Third, maternal custody allowed an exchange relationship to develop between mothers and their children. Were children to be in the custody of their fathers, the children's sense of obligation to their mothers would be considerably weakened. In the mother's custody children might be counted on to contribute to the long-term support of their mothers, thus relieving taxpayers of a potential burden associated with supporting divorced women.

Fourth, this was nearly a no-lose political solution. Maternal preference was favored both by many conservative legislators and by many feminists. Conservatives favored the solution for many reasons, but in part because it restricted the welfare obligations of the state. Many feminists favored the solution because it lowered the cost of divorce for women and, at the same time, might be taken as evidence of increased legal rights.

Finally, taken together, the benefits offered by this solution gave it a certain rough justice: it made the guilty party pay for the divorce. After all, why should the burden of a failed marriage—and a disrupted family—fall on every taxpayer's shoulders? What they failed to anticipate was that divorce would go from being a rare event to a highly probable event in the life of each man, woman, and child. As the divorce rate grew beyond all expectations, custody laws that once dealt with the exceptional would come to regulate the common divorce case. An institutional arrangement designed for the few soon became one applied to the many. Law for deviants became law for ordinary citizens.

However, in most cases the law did not specify mothers. What it did do was to give judges absolute discretionary powers in matters of custody. It is not difficult to understand why paternal custody was the norm prior to the shift: the father's rights and obligations bound him to the child. Yet the norm of maternal custody is nearly as extreme as the norm of paternal custody once was, and the period of transition was really quite short, given the pervasiveness of the change. No social revolution arose that might explain the shift. Why, then, the extremes of preference?

Exaggerated distributions of custody awards are a function of the aggregation of individual custody decisions. How this happens is easily seen in successive flips of a biased coin. Whereas in the long run an unbiased coin will yield a roughly equal number of heads and tails, a biased one will, in the long run, produce an extreme outcome (for example, 80% heads, 20% tails). The coin need only be slightly biased to produce the highly skewed distribution. The situation is similar for judges. Consider a judge who has but the slightest preference for maternal over paternal custody.[3] In each decision where the evidence suggests that both parties will make reasonable custodians, his slight bias will lead him to make a judgment of maternal custody. Taken collectively, his decisions will appear to reveal an extreme preference for maternal custody.

Thus, it would be a mistake to assume that a preference for one parent as against another ever required the edifice of a complete social ideology. In fact, it is necessary only to have a slight preference for one or another outcome, a slight normative bias. In this way, modest changes in social climate can produce profound differences in outcome (such as 85% of all children being awarded to their mothers following divorce after a period of predominantly paternal custody). Whereas the explanation given above for the change in preference is a social explanation to explain a social fact, judges need not subscribe to, or even be aware of, those causes. They need only catch the shifts in the wind of normative and institutional changes.

Were guides for awarding custody a matter of public policy rather than prompts in the arena of judicial discretion, more explicit public debates regarding the preferred distribution, or even the idea of custody itself, might become necessary. But as long as the discretion given judges and divorcing parents is considerable—in the name of the best interests of the children—no sustained public discussion of the merits of custody either as an institution or as a description of a distribution of awards is likely.

Nonetheless, the social bargain between parents and their children is under review. The condition of children generally and of divorced children in particular is of growing concern.

Reassessing the Social Bargain

What is the proper way to begin to think about the condition of children, particularly children of divorce? Minow and Weissbourd (1993) outline the dimensions of the problems children face:

> There has been much made in recent years about the millions of American children growing up in single-parent homes, or traumatized by divorce. Only recently, however, have the dimensions of this problem started to come into view. In the past thirty years . . . the divorce rate has tripled; so has the percentage of children across the nation living with only one parent. Since 75 percent of divorced mothers and 80 percent of divorced fathers remarry, and since the divorce rate in remarriages is higher than in first marriages, many children must not only ride out one divorce, but must navigate through the stormy seas of remarriage, only then to be knocked off course by a second divorce. As of two years after a divorce, contact with fathers falls off precipitously—only 16 percent of all children will see their fathers at least once a week, and nearly 50 percent will have no contact with their fathers at all. Fathers will be entirely absent from the lives of almost 66 percent of these children ten years after the divorce.

It would be remarkable, indeed, if children were unaffected by these dramatic life changes. The commonest way to assess the postdivorce condition of children is to compare their well-being on a variety of dimensions with those of children from intact families. If divorce had no effect on children's well-being, the variation among children of divorce and among children of intact families on a variety of economic, social, and psychological measures would be greater than their between-group variation.

Yet this is not the case. Furstenberg and Cherlin (1991) report that unless they remarry, many women live in or near poverty, meaning that "for women and children . . . every year a million families experience a drop in income that is similar to what families went through during the Great Depression" (p. 53). Further, "divorced women and their children do not regain their predivorce standard of living until five years after the breakup, on average" (Furstenberg and Cherlin 1991, p. 52). The sharpest drop in standard of living is experienced by those who were married to men with substantial incomes. Among those children in families covered by child-support agreements, one quarter of noncustodial fathers pay nothing, while the amount paid by others is almost certainly inadequate. The assured-child support plan authored by Garfinkel (1994), instituted in some measure in half of the states, may alleviate some of the burden on children whose fathers are economically more advantaged. But it is unlikely to have any effect on poor children.

The most serious economic problem comes from the most basic fact of divorce: splitting what was once a common pie. No matter what the family income prior to divorce, and no matter how demanding the level of child support, dividing the same income among two households will necessarily lead to a lower standard of living.

Psychological troubles of varying degrees are evident in children of divorce, although many of the studies use small, non-representative samples, and violate numerous methodological tenets (see Demo and Acock 1988). Wallerstein (1983, 1984, 1985) reports evidence of long-lasting psychological effects in some children and summarizes literature suggesting that children of divorce are overrepresented in outpatient psychiatric, family agency, and private practice patient populations.

In the short term, Solnit (1983) argues that parental separation and divorce are always experienced by children as a threat to their well-being, self-esteem, and security, although the expression of these emotions depends on age and experience. Short-term negative effects on adjustment are fairly well established (Hetherington, Cox, and Cox 1979; Kurdek, Blisk, and Siesky 1981; Wallerstein and Kelly 1975, 1980). Older children are more likely to adjust than are younger children (Kurdek and Siesky 1980), although general behavioral problems among adolescents (Peterson and Zill 1986) as well as actual delinquent behavior (Dornbusch et al. 1985) are more evident in those who come from broken as against intact families.

Boys seem to be more disadvantaged in their adjustments, measured along dimensions of both severity and length (Hetherington 1979; Hetherington et al. 1978, 1979, 1982; Wallerstein 1984; Wallerstein and Kelley 1980).

Turning to measures related to school performance, there is some evidence to suggest that elementary school children are worse off than are preschool children, at least as measured by their school behavior (Kinard and Reinherz 1984, 1986). Cognitive well-being also suffers: there is an inverse relationship between academic achievement and general cognitive performance and familial disruption and conflict (Hess and Camara 1979; Kinard and Reinherz 1986; Kurdek 1981; Radin 1981; Shinn 1978).

Although the robustness of any one of these results is probably open to question (see Furstenberg and Cherlin 1991 for cautionary admonitions), taken together they suggest that there are significant differences in well-being between children of divorce and children from intact families. The gravity of the situation comes not so much from the differences themselves, but from the question that can be inferred from those differences: would these children who suffer the ill-effects of divorce have had more advantageous childhoods had their parents not divorced?

Minow and Weissbourd (1993) offer a particularly cogent discussion of children and divorce, one that cuts to the quick:

> Divorce is not, of course, always a negative experience for children. Divorce may rescue children from a miserable and destructive home situation created by warring parents. . . . Yet divorce also imposes large costs for millions of children, both immediately and over time. Immediately following the divorce, many children find themselves filled with anger, resentment, depression, and anxiety. Helplessness often overwhelms them. Many children infer that they cannot control events that deeply affect their lives. . . . Divorce may also fundamentally change the way children think about the future and impair their abilities to form lasting relationships and to love. . . . Children from divorced families must often deal with the loss of one parent and also the potentially unstable status of their custodial parent. . . . Children share the difficulties of their parents following a divorce and may also become caught in their parents' cycles of suffering. . . . Precisely when both children and custodial parents need their familiar anchors, they suffer disruptive changes. (pp. 3–5)

These results give rise to the following question: are there alternative custody arrangements that would better serve the needs of children? Empirical evidence supporting one custodial arrangement as against another is scanty (Furstenberg and Cherlin 1991). Yet, the weight of the evidence that postdivorce custodial arrangements, whatever they may be, are not producing positive effects for children or their parents has prompted discussion of policy alternatives. The following section reviews various child custody alternatives to sole maternal custody in light of the sociohistorical analysis of institutions of child custody.

What to Do? Assessments of Proposed Child Custody Alternatives

Increasingly there are challenges to the current system of custody assignment. Some question the fairness of the system to one parent or another. Others seek to constrain judicial discretion. I will consider a set of those proposals, including those that seek to discover the better parent, that encourage parents to decide between themselves, that let states vet parental agreements, that leave the decision to a flip of a coin, that give automatic sole custody to mothers, and that give preference to primary caretakers.

King Solomon and the True Parent

The story of Solomon (1 *Kings* 3:16–28) often serves as a powerful metaphor for discussions of child custody dilemmas following divorce (see, for example, Elster 1989). To discover the true mother of the disputed infant, Solomon proposed to cut the child in two. The story tells us that Solomon believed that his threat would reveal the true mother for she would sooner give up her child than allow it to be killed.

The power of the metaphor comes from several aspects of the story. First, Solomon discovers what he believes to be a preference-revealing device associated with observable behavior. The true mother would rush forward to save the child's life, and observers would then know that her altruism was stronger than her self-interest. Second, the story is consistent with the venue in which custody decisions are presently made: in all disputed custody cases where both parents can make a credible claim for custody, the outcome rests with a single decision-maker, the judge. (Who, everyone hopes, has the wisdom of Solomon.) Third, the mood of the story is one of passion and violence, thereby capturing the sentiment of most disputed custody cases, past and present.

Yet the metaphor misleads. Were there a true preference-revealing device, judges would surely use it, particularly if it could separate the altruistic from the selfish parent. Even parents might be grateful for such a device if each believed that he or she was truly the most committed parent. Unfortunately, there is no magical—or scientific—method. Individuals often do not know their own preferences. Additionally, those preferences can change. The preferences of the mother and father in a contested custody battle are not the preferences of the husband and wife who lovingly decided to jointly produce that child, even though they are, in fact, the same people.[4]

Solomon had an enviable task compared to that of judges now deciding custody. Solomon was required to adjudicate between a true and a false claim. Judges must decide between two true parents, two truthful claims to parenthood. That this story has served as a powerful metaphor captures a subtle but important feature of current custody debates: the attempt of the legal and scholarly communities to elevate one parental claim above another as a way of deciding between two true parents

(Goldstein, Freud, and Solnit 1979a, 1979b). The result of this process may be to make one of the parents *seem* truer than the other. But unlike in the story, the distinction is at heart not authentic.

The metaphor is inappropriate for another reason, as well. The story is recounted, but removed from its historical context. How are we to understand why the claim of the false mother was at all a credible one? Why was Solomon's threat to kill the child believable? In what sort of social structure might a false and a true mother seek adjudication over a disputed child?[5] And what sort of legal system would permit a judge's sentence of death over an innocent child to resolve a contest between two adults? The part of the story that is never told is crucial: the child in dispute was illegitimate and both of the women were of questionable moral character, women who lived outside of the community's laws and mores.

For all of these reasons, we must move beyond Solomonic imagery.

Negotiated Resolution in Child Custody, Vetted by the State

The indeterminacy of the best-interest principle is of concern on several grounds. Whereas the flaw of determinate outcomes is fairness, the flaw of indeterminacy is the concomitant ambiguous incentive structure. Robert Mnookin suggests that this might be overcome, to some extent, by private party resolution: "indeed, for any private custody dispute, the primary implication of the indeterminacy of the best-interests standard is that the legal process should encourage the parties themselves to work out their own resolution" (Mnookin 1975, p. 292).

When parents do work out their own resolution, they are engaged in two-party bargaining where it is likely that norms of equitable distribution prevail. But what do parents have to work with to achieve equitable distribution? The child is indivisible, and so:

> Divorcing parents often negotiate and agree about child custody while simultaneously settling other issues such as visitation, child support, and marital property division. *The eventual agreement about custody may often be a reflection of the parents' interests in these other matters, rather than the child's.* (Mnookin 1975, p. 288, emphasis added)

In these negotiations, parents are simultaneously principals and agents (for their children). In a contest between their own interests and those of their children, it is axiomatic that their own interests will hold sway. This, in itself, might reveal certain sorts of preferences; it is useful to know which parent will exchange the child for the house.

> Nevertheless, as an operating rule, it seems plain that a negotiated resolu-
> tion is preferable from the child's perspective for several reasons. Since a
> child's social and psychological relationships with *both* parents ordinarily
> continue after the divorce, a process that leads to agreement between the
> parents is preferable to one that necessarily has a winner and a loser.
> (Mnookin 1975, p. 288)

Yet this advantage for parents—no losers, no absolute winners—may
entail a loss for their children, as their welfare is partitioned among their
parents. That each of the parents may experience greater well-being is
irrelevant to the issue of whether either of them has agreed to take
responsibility—as separate from custody—for addressing the needs of
their children. The usual sort of settlement is one in which needs are
partitioned, and so no one takes full responsibility. Although this has
the aura of fairness for the parents, it does not solve the problems
inherent in providing for children: the very structure of bargaining promotes the diffusion of responsibility among parents.

There may be an underlying assumption here that a more satisfied
parent is one who is more likely to contribute. But both theoretical analysis and empirical observation suggest strongly that sentiment is an insufficient condition on which to base the security of children.

This analysis suggests then that it is not the indeterminacy of the best
interest principle that leads to diminution of children's welfare. Instead
it is the model by which parents bargain and negotiate according to their
interests and needs that results in a lower level of children's welfare.

It would be possible to keep an indeterminate best-interest principle,
but institute a winner-take-all decision rule: the parent who takes custody assumes all obligations toward the children. The structure of bargaining supporting this sort of decision rule would be akin to a method used
in difficult labor–management negotiations: final-offer arbitration. In
this type of bargaining structure, each side presents a contract specifying
both their obligations as well as those of the other party. The arbitrator is
compelled to accept one of them without amendment. Applying this in
the case of custody settlements following divorce, each parent would
present to the judge a complete divorce settlement that included proposed custodial provisions. This would offer each parent an opportunity
to express the extent of his or her postdivorce commitment to the child
in the context of the new economic social and familial structure.[6] Judges
would then be bound to select the settlement proposal that comes clos-
est to meeting the best-interests criterion, without the judge having to
decide on any of the specific terms. Thus, it would satisfy Mnookin's
intuition that parents must know—better than judges—what the best
interests of their children are.

Joint Custody

On the face of it, joint custody seems to be an equitable solution to the problem of dividing the child. Even when physical custody is not shared, under an arrangement of joint legal custody each parent maintains some interest in the child and control over decisions affecting the child's welfare:

> The distinguishing feature of joint custody is that both parents retain legal responsibility and authority for the care and control of the child, much as in an intact family. Joint custody upon divorce is defined here as an arrangement in which both parents have equal rights and responsibilities regarding major decisions and neither parent's rights are superior. Joint custody basically means providing each parent with an equal voice in the children's education upbringing, religious training, nonemergency medical care, and general welfare. (Folberg 1984, p. 7)

This picture suggests that parents whose conflicts or incompatibility are so great as to necessitate divorce are somehow able to manage to concur on a joint path of raising their children. It is not surprising to learn that among those who settled on joint custody, over time only one-fourth were able to cooperate in parenting (Maccoby and Mnookin 1992). Instead, more common patterns included continuing conflictual parenting relations or disengaged parallel parenting (the child shuttles between two homes, but the parents do not communicate with one another regularly and therefore do not attempt to coordinate their efforts). Without coordination, and without a structure in which each parent has the means to compel the other to engage in appropriate behaviors and make investments in their children, joint custody is hardly akin to an intact family.

Joint custody is at least as likely as alternative custody arrangements are to result in diffusion of responsibility for the child. When both take responsibility, it is tantamount to neither doing so. Why should one parent provide when the other parent has promised to do so? If they agree to partition those responsibilities, joint custody is no different than a traditional arrangement, and is subject to the same criticisms.

Primary Caretaker Presumption and the Motherhood Model

The primary caretaker presumption is predicated on two principles (Chambers 1984). The first is that it provides continuity for children: the person who has provided the most care during marriage should be the one to provide principal care following marriage. The second is that it is fair because it rewards the parent who has devoted the most to the child during the marriage. While there may be some disagreement among parents as to who the primary caretaker was during marriage, the disagreement is not substantial (Maccoby and Mnookin 1992). At present, a primary caretaker assumption is tantamount to a motherhood principle (Mason 1991), for caretaking is in most cases defined as mothering.

The preceding historical analysis suggests that as long as fathers continue to provide material support, mothers' interests and state's interests are joined in a motherhood principle. The recent enactments of Child Support Acts—seeking to recover child support payments from delinquent fathers and instituting procedures for the automatic garnishment of wages of noncustodial fathers—are borne from this alliance of mothers and states.

Yet both the primary caretaker presumption, as well as the refined motherhood model, utilize too narrow a definition of what caretaking means. It is not just that mothers often work and consign their children to others for caretaking, it is that caretaking depends upon financial provision and education as much as it depends on those duties that define nurture. The primary caretaker definition offered by Chambers (1984, p. 562)—"the parent . . . who has performed a substantial majority of the caregiving tasks for the child that involve intimate interaction with the child"—ignores the fact that there must be food to feed the child, garments with which to clothe the child, and a bed to tuck her into. *Providing food, clothing, and shelter are primary, not secondary, functions of parenthood.*

To meet the needs of children, primary caretaking would have to take into account all necessary obligations, not just those of nurture. To do this, however, would challenge the motherhood model or would necessitate significant social changes:

> A motherhood model would focus on making the workplace work for mothers and children. The persistent wage gap, caused in large part by the low wage structure of female occupations and part-time work, can be tackled by a combination of comparable worth legislation and old-fashioned collective bargaining. Working conditions can and should be altered to meet the needs of mothers, who are now a major factor in the workforce. Maternity leaves, family sickness leaves, flex-time and part-time tracks should become as accepted as the eight hour day. (Mason 1991, p. 50)

However, in the absence of these sorts of social changes, the full range of obligations to children cannot be met by a motherhood model.

Randomization of Custody Awards

Both Mnookin (1975) and Elster (1989) discuss the possibility of the randomization of custody awards through some probabilistic procedure such as coin tossing. Its appeal comes from its apparent fairness in deciding between two fit parents and its efficiency in avoiding prolonged adjudication.

Its strength, however, comes not from its postdivorce advantages, but from its implications for parental behavior within marriage. For two committed parents, tossing a coin may be associated with the best incentive structure for parenting prior to divorce, especially if both perceive a gender bias against their own gender in the legal system. If they imagine that custody will be awarded through such a procedure following divorce—presuming roughly equally desirable parents—then they have an incentive to develop as close a relationship as possible with their children. If they do not divorce, they benefit from this strategy; if they do, they have at least an equal chance of being awarded sole custody.

Mnookin (1975) suspects that this would be an objectionable procedure, and that "the repulsion that many would probably feel towards this suggestion may reflect an intuitive appreciation of the importance of the educational, participatory, and symbolic values of adjudication as a mode of dispute settlement" (p. 291). Yet a less lofty explanation suffices to account for its absence as a strategy of custody resolution. It cannot satisfy the state's interests for it fails to address the question of how to provide for divorced mothers. And like other proposed solutions, it throws into question the range of obligation associated with custody. If it does not necessarily include financial obligation, for instance, and if custody were to be decided by the flip of a coin, why not financial obligation, as well?

Problems Common to These Solutions

The principle that was to guide judicial decisions following the transition from paternal preference in custody to maternal preference in custody—the best interests of children—turned out to offer a wide berth of judicial discretion but little in the way of guidance. Best interests are subject to considerable dispute and interpretation. More than this, however, focusing on the presumed best interests of the children fails to take into account other operative, and often predominant, interests of fathers, mothers, and the state. The present dilemmas of custody awards as well as the proposals just considered are weakened by their failure to take conflicting interests into account, and by further assuming that best interests are sufficient to overcome any potential conflicts.

Further, these solutions all focus on parents, and are concerned particularly with issues of equity. Is the bargain fair to each parent? Are mothers rewarded for their efforts in attending to the daily needs of their children during the marriage? Does the solution have at least the appearance of equity? These may be important issues, but they are secondary to the needs of children. Dividing material resources does not specify how the material needs of children are to be met, even if it is, in fact, fair to the two parties to the bargain. Dividing the child's time, as in a joint physical custody arrangement, does not specify who will take responsibility for ensuring that the child gets the best possible education.

The preference for mothers, implicitly or explicitly upheld in each of these proposals, also gives preference to nurturing over material support. Yet nurture is the one aspect of parenting that needs the least legal support, for it is the least problematic, owing more to sentiment than to interest. Whereas parental love has proven to be a weak basis on which to predicate a system of attending to children's security needs, it is a much stronger prompt to nurture. In part this is because love and affection is the one area in which the child can give as much as he or she gets, so that exchange dominates this part of the relationship between parent and child. Further, love and affection are nearly boundless resources, unlike material resources, which are scarce. Children can compete far more effectively for emotional resources than material ones. Therefore, the child's affectional needs are much more likely to be given their due than the child's material needs.

Another weakness of these proposals is that they assume that the behaviors of mothers and fathers toward their children in marriage are good indicators of their future, postdivorce behavior toward their children. This assumption fails to take into account the link between structure and behavior. An intact family may embody an incentive structure such that a gender-specific division of labor frequently arises (Becker 1981, 1991). Observing that women in intact families specialize in the upbringing of children or that men invest in outside employment to support their families is to be interpreted not so much as preference, but as a collective response to the extant incentive structure. To assume that the preferences will remain when the structure producing them has disappeared is unwarranted.

In the postdivorce family, there is limited possibility for specialization, and hardly any motivation for it. Noncustodial fathers can be compelled to provide financial resources, but they no longer benefit from that contribution as they did in the intact family. By the presence of their children custodial mothers still provide daily care, but the postdivorce structure is likely to push them into paid labor, as well. Is it their preference to attend less singularly to nurturing their children? Perhaps yes, perhaps no. The point is that the postdivorce structure changes their behavior, and so to assume that their behavior in the predivorce family is a good guide to their postdivorce behavior, even with respect to their children, is unwarranted.

Finally, these solutions pay too little attention to the question of social control with respect to provisioning children. Whereas the intact family has an informal, although powerful, endogenous system of control, after divorce, there are few controls on parents' behaviors. To expect the state to enforce agreements is both too difficult and too costly. Only in cases of the most blatant disregard for children's basic welfare can states be expected to intervene.

To be effective in meeting children's needs following divorce, custodial arrangements must focus explicitly on those needs, and how to meet them. First those needs must be enunciated once again, as Blackstone did two hundred years ago. Second, arrangements for meeting those needs must take into account competing interests of parents and their children, issues of social control, and the link between structure and behavior. Third, adults must come to terms with the possibility that meeting children's needs following divorce may preclude meeting their own.

A Child-Centric Alternative

The question that has been asked in custody—Who gets this child?—is simply the wrong question. The right question is—Who wants the obligations for this child? But before turning to the question of how custody determinations would be decided if this were to be the guiding question, a prior question must be asked: should unconstrained divorce be possible?

Should Unconstrained Divorce Be Possible?

For the reasons set out in the first chapter, the intact family is structurally superior, from the child's point of view, to the divorced one. This is because children are collective goods, and even their parents may underinvest in them unless they are constrained by the other parent not to do so. In the absence of the other parent, due to divorce, there is no incentive for maximum investment; indeed, there is an incentive to try to shift responsibility to the other parent. Additionally, parents are agents for their children and it is axiomatic that agents will follow their own interests as against those of the principals they represent when there are competing interests. Agency is more constrained in an intact family than in a divorced one.

For these reasons, it is worth reconsidering possible limitations on divorce during the period of childhood. Limitations on divorce have not been a serious subject of policy debate for the past 70 years. Nonetheless, this analysis strongly points to a reconsideration, even in the face of its political infeasibility.

The contractual basis of marriage leads, as Regan (1993) argues, to an orientation that marriages are dispensable when they no longer satisfy the needs and desires of the spouses. For many adults, alternatives abound, and new marriages are contracted. There are faults in this system for adults (Regan 1993), but it is a system that is deeply flawed for children, who do not enjoy the same set of alternatives that adults do.

Given the disjuncture between the costs of divorce for children and the costs of divorce for adults, a two-tiered system of divorce law might be imagined. Without children, adults would be free to divorce at will, as they now do. Once there were children, however, the basis of marriage would change from a contractual one to a status one, where the adults' principal legal identities would change from freely contracting individuals to parents. As parents of children under 18, in order to divorce, they would be called on to demonstrate that the *family* was better off broken than intact. Unhappiness with one's spouse would not then be a compelling argument for divorce. Domestic violence would be. At the end of childhood, the status of parents would revert again to that of freely contracting adults, with the privilege of unconstrained divorce.

The political infeasibility of this solution is the result of its emphasis on children's welfare *as against* adult's welfare. In a sense, that is precisely the point. When adults decide to divorce, it is their own welfare that they have in mind. If it is truly the case that children are also served by the decision to divorce, then that can be demonstrated to the court, and divorce granted.

Adults are also the legislators and voters, and are unlikely to bind themselves to a system that so clearly constrains their choices. Suppose, however, that such a system were in place. What incentives would follow? The most obvious would be that one might not be any more careful about whom one married, but one would certainly be more careful about whom one decided to have children with. There is no doubt but that any, even slight, movement in the direction of reflective childbearing would be advantageous to children. Under a system of constrained divorce, one would make an 18-year commitment with the first child, and would extend that commitment with every child thereafter. Given average life expectancy, that period still does not cover the majority of adulthood, but it is roughly two and a half times greater than the average duration of marriage.

For some adults—those who miscalculate in their choice—life would be unhappier. The long period of history in which divorce was unavailable would, however, suggest that adults would find ways to make accommodations. Those accommodations—including infidelity—are not, in themselves, as harmful to children as is divorce. That is because the resources of the family are unaffected by these accommodations, and the status of parents is upheld.

The more dependent, less powerful spouse might have a greater incentive to want children in order to protect the marriage for his or her own well-being. Yet that is the case now, as well. That this might not be the purest motivation for having children is irrelevant from the point of view of the children who are born. A system of constrained divorce would protect both those children and the less powerful spouse. More powerful spouses would have an incentive to use their power more carefully.

A system of child-centric constrained divorce also has implications for nontraditional families. Adopting children would produce the same legal effect on adopting parents as on biological ones. If children are to be adopted by same-sex parents, those individuals should be permitted to bind themselves through marriage as heterosexuals do. And they should be constrained similarly with respect to divorce.

Would this encourage women *who would otherwise have married* to have children out of wedlock? The challenges of raising children are probably sufficient to encourage most women to seek partners. But if this were not the case, under the proposed system there might be two further constraints, one economic and one normative. Economic incentives— through taxes—might be used to dissuade women from bearing children out of wedlock. Beyond this, however, if such a system were in place, a shift in normative equilibrium would occur: the great majority of children would be raised by two parents throughout their childhood. Raising a child alone, by choice, would again become a normative aberration, and subject to social sanctions.

This proposal is not merely a return to the old ways. The old ways constrained divorce for adults for moral and religious reasons. This is a proposal that places the needs of children above the desires of adults, and constrains adults' behavior to meet children's needs. Still, it is highly improbable that such a plan will ever be a matter for public policy debate, for it clearly contravenes adults' individual interests. Therefore, I turn toward a consideration of alternative principles by which to award custody.

Awarding Custody following Divorce

What sort of custodial arrangement follows from the forgoing theoretical and historical analysis? Turning to the question of obligations for the child (rather than the divisibility of the child) changes the content of the decision substantially. The key is to turn to the discussion from what parents get to what parents give. "Who wants responsibility for this child?" in contested custody cases embodies several questions. What are the needs of the child? What arrangements does each parent plan to make to address these needs? Which is the superior plan? And, finally, what control mechanisms are available for ensuring compliance?

Children need material support, education, and nurture. How might the court determine which parent is prepared to make the greatest investment in the child? There are several reasons to ask parents to *specify* their commitment to the child's material well-being and education. The first reason is that, upon award of custody, their specifications would constitute a legally binding contract. Courts would do well to specify the terms of this contract. Where will the child live? What school will the child attend? What arrangements will be made for after-school care? (Or, if the child is an infant, what provisions will be made for caretaking?) What are the parent's behavioral goals for the child (including attainment in school, enrichment activities, and the like), and what commitments will be made to help the child to reach these goals? For children whose class position warrants it, what provisions do parents plan to make for college?

The second reason is that the answers to these questions would provide a basis of comparison between two acceptable parents, and would allow a third party to measure which parent was willing to make the greater investment in the child. Children's present welfare and future welfare are enhanced by greater investment. Sociological understanding rarely speaks with one voice, but, in this case, it does: life chances are constrained by material and educational advantages. Children who are more advantaged simply have better opportunities to maximize their present and future well-being.

It will be noted that nurture is not subject to specification. There are several reasons for this. First, it is difficult to measure. Second, for reasons that I have discussed above, children are in a better position to demand—and get—emotional support from their parents than they are to get material or educational support.

Furthermore, even though the commitment to nurture remains unmeasured, the parent's specification of commitments to support and educate provides an important preference-revealing mechanism. The proposed investment in the child is an indication of the extent of the parent's willingness to forgo alternative investments that might have more directly self-interested benefits. Love is revealed in doing rather than professing.

In making a bid for custody by specifying their plans to meet a set of obligations to their child, parents are constrained by their personal and material resources. At the same time, their bid reflects their interest in and willingness to parent. If, for example, fathers are not willing to part with their greater resources, as many suspect they are not, then mothers will offer the more attractive proposal to meet obligations and will win the custody of their children.

There is an interesting problem that arises when there are substantial asymmetries of parental endowments. Let us suppose that we have a case of a rich father and a poor mother. In this instance, it is much easier for the father to make the winning bid for custody. As long as his proposed investments exceed the mother's, he wins. Yet the proportion of his discretionary resources that he is willing to bid may be less than the proportion of her discretionary resources that the mother is willing to bid. If proportionality were the indirect measure of desire or willing-ness to parent, then the mother ought to win. Yet even in this case, it is both in the child's interests and the state's interests that absolute advan-tage hold sway. Both are better off when a greater investment is made in the child. Furthermore, the father need not have made a proposal at all.

There will be considerable variation in parental asymmetries. Some of these will result in unequal proposals. Others will not. Should each parent offer a roughly equal commitment to meet the obligations to the child, let the primary caretaker preference then be the deciding factor.

Finally, this kind of approach to awarding custody can also accommo-date a situation in which parents want to jointly provide for their child and can agree upon a plan to do so. However, unlike current joint custody arrangements in which the focus is on equal voice on matters of childrearing, a joint custody plan under this system would specify the obligations of each parent toward their child.

Whereas joint custody specifies both parents' obligations, there is no reason that sole custody awards under this proposal should have any implications for the continuing child support obligations of the noncus-todial parent. Anything that increases investment in the child is desir-able. Thus, the progress that has been made in the area of defining a minimum standard of contribution of the noncustodial parent, as well as the child assurance plans, should be preserved.

The advantages of this sort of proposal over current arrangements derive from two features: the criteria governing the custodial parent's behavior are observable and measurable, and it promotes the maximum volitional investment in the child.

Enforcing Custody Arrangements

Intact families have an endogenous enforcement mechanism to pro-vide for the welfare of the child. Divorce and the current system of custody destroy this enforcement mechanism by increasing parental control costs. This leads to increased parental free riding with respect to the child. The state is incapable of enforcing proper parental behavior—due to excessive social control costs—unless parental behavior falls below a very low minimum standard (e.g., young children left unattended, unfed, beaten). How might the plan enunciated above circumvent these social control problems?

Enforcement is possible only when commitments are measurable, publicly stated, and legally binding. Thus, the first advantage of the plan is that the commitments of the custodial parent are public, measurable, and legally binding. In the current situation, only the *noncustodial* parent's obligations have these characteristics (e.g., child support payments).

Still the question arises of how to enforce these commitments. There are at least two ways. To minimize state social control costs, the most efficient method is to encourage regular visitation with the noncustodial parent. This parent—having lost the bid for custody—is likely to be a keen observer of compliance. Challenges to the custodial arrangement would be heard by the court in cases where the custodial parent was not meeting his or her obligations to the child, set forth in the custodial plan. Regular visitation makes the noncustodial parent the informal agent of social control.[7] This is as close to the endogenous social control arrangement characteristic of the intact family as is possible in a divorced one.

Using the noncustodial parent as the informal agent of social control has a harsh edge, but it is the custodial parent's compliance with stated commitments that serves the child. An advantageous custody plan with no enforcement mechanism has little chance of survival in the face of competing interests.

Regular visitation may be infeasible, however. The noncustodial parent's interest in the child may wane, geographic distance may separate the child and the noncustodial parent, or the ex-spouses may find it too uncomfortable to maintain sustained contact, even if it benefits the child. Without regular visitation, enforcement falls to the state.

Why do states have an interest in enforcing custody contracts? A weak reason is that it is one of the state's primary functions to enforce contracts. A slightly stronger reason is that when parents fail to meet their obligations to their children, states generally intervene, albeit only in the most extreme instances of neglect of parental duties. The most compelling reason is offered by Coleman (1993, p. 13):

> There is . . . one actor with strong interests in maximizing a child's value to society, or minimizing its cost. This is the state. The costs of undeveloped human capital (and conversely the benefits of its development)

accrue to governments: costs of schooling; costs of crime (including the cost of apprehending and incarcerating criminals); costs of welfare payments; medical costs induced by lifestyles; costs associated with alcohol and drug use; and finally, on the other side of the ledger, benefits from income taxes.

Although Coleman's argument is meant to apply to all children, it is applicable in the specific instance of children of divorce. Whereas the relationship between the state and parents in intact families is quite ambiguous, it is less so in the case of divorce. All children of divorce are in the state's jurisdiction until custody is awarded. The state thus has an advantage in the case of divorce that it does not have with respect to intact families: it can specify the private parties' obligation—the parents' obligation—to the children in whom it has a compelling interest.

How might the state enforce such contracts? One possibility might require custodial parents to file evaluation reports on a regular basis. These reports would include measures of compliance with the contractual stipulations as well as child evaluation indicators (school progress reports, for instance). Significant deviations from the original commitments as well as notable declines in the well-being of child might then be cause for action. To enforce parental obligations would mark the logical conclusion of the state's gradual assumption of parental rights, at least in the case of divorce.

Other Considerations

Is the proposed plan fair? The question is, of course, fair to whom? When divorcing parents are equally interested in winning custody of their child, the plan clearly advantages the parent with greater resources. Given the unequal position of women in the labor market, this would disadvantage mothers relative to fathers. It is, then, potentially unfair to women. An optimistic view is that this asymmetry would lead to important social changes such as comparable pay, workplace responsiveness to parental requirements, and the like. A pessimistic view is that women, who already suffer more substantial financial losses in divorce than do men (Weitzman 1985), would suffer more substantial emotional losses, as well. If part of women's disadvantage owes to their greater contribution to childrearing during marriage, they then bear the consequences of a kind of double jeopardy.

Yet children cannot and should not serve as the salve for society's various injustices. That is the difference between a child-centric and an adult-centric approach to child custody.

There is a final matter. Should children have separate legal representation to defend their interests? It might be supposed that the child-centric stance adopted herein would advocate for separate legal counsel. Yet it is precisely this child-centric stance that suggests that the answer to this question is no. That is because children have no greater capacity than adults do to bind themselves to the mast. By this I mean that what children require most to bring them to their full capacities as adults is consistent authoritative parenting, replete with careful monitoring and sanctioning of their behavior toward others, at school, and at home. It would be the rare child who could anticipate this as his or her greatest want.

Circumventing the Structure of Indifference

The most disastrous consequence emanating from the change from a preference for fathers in custody to a preference for mothers in custody around the turn of the century was the establishment of a structure of indifference to the child's holistic well-being following divorce. That this was unintentional cannot be emphasized sufficiently: it was not that fathers were interested in their children's welfare in its entirety because of their superiority as parents, but rather because this was the structure of paternal obligation. It is this structure that emphasized responsibility for the child that was superior to the current morass, not paternal custody itself. The essential point is that the separation of the responsibilities that bound a single agent to the child at the time of the transition from paternal to maternal custody may have led to a situation in which no one takes *primary* responsibility for the child of divorce.

What Maisie Knew

If we hope to circumvent the structure of indifference, we must take to heart what Maisie knew. Because divorce is a highly emotionally charged event, it is full of self-delusions, justifications, and strategic moves. Social science has trailed behind literature in its appreciation of the layered, murky, human character of divorce. What Maisie knew was that, despite the impassioned rhetoric of both her mother and father, each claiming to represent her true best interests, neither of them was ultimately motivated by concern for her, but rather for themselves:

> The child was provided for, but the new arrangement was inevitably confounding to a young intelligence intensely aware that something had happened which must matter a good deal and looking out for the effects of so

great a cause. It was to be the fate of this patient little girl to see much more than she at first understood, but also even at first to understand much more than any little girl, however patient, had perhaps ever understood before. Only a drummer-boy in a ballad or a story could have been so in the thick of the fight. She was taken into the confidence of the passions on which she fixed just the stare she might have had for images bounding across the wall in the slide of a magic lantern. Her little world was phantasmagoric—strange shadows dancing on a sheet. It was as if the whole performance had been given for her—a mite of a half-scared infant in a great dim theatre. She was in short introduced to a life with a liberality in which the selfishness of others found its account, and there was nothing to avert the sacrifice but the modesty of her youth. (James 1897, p. 39)

In this passage Henry James offers those of us who seek to practice social science in this terrain a cautionary tale. One must look beneath the words of those who would speak for children. This is a methodological warning, but it has far-reaching substantive implications. When adults chant incantations and wave their wands of power all in the name of children's interests: Beware!

'Poor little monkey!' she at last exclaimed; and the words were an epitaph for the tomb of Maisie's childhood. She was abandoned to her fate. What was clear to any spectator was that the only link binding her to either parent was this lamentable fact of her being a ready vessel for bitterness, a deep little porcelain cup in which biting acids could be mixed. They had wanted her not for any good they could do her, but for the harm they could, with her unconscious aid, do each other. She should serve their anger and seal their revenge, for husband and wife had been alike crippled by the heavy hand of justice, which in the last resort met on neither side their indignant claim to get, as they called it, everything. If each was only to get half this seemed to concede that neither was so base as the other pretended, or to put it differently, offered them both as bad indeed, since they were only as good as each other. The mother had wished to prevent the father from, as she said, 'so much as looking' at the child; the father's plea was that the mother's lightest touch was 'simply contamination'. These were the opposed principles in which Maisie was to be educated— she fit them together as she might. Nothing could have been more touching at first than her failure to suspect the ordeal that awaited her little unspotted soul. (James 1897, pp. 36–37)

Notes

1.   The other two are audience inhibition and social influence. The former refers to the process by which a bystander who decides to intervene runs the risk of embarrassment and negative evaluation by others if the situation was misin-

terpreted and was not really cause for intervention. Social influence refers to the fact that situations may be ambiguous and so individuals look to others to help define it. The presence of others inhibits intervention if individuals see the inaction of others as a sign that the situation is less critical or that inaction is the expected norm. Audience inhibition and social influence exert independent effects on social inhibition (Latane and Darley 1976; Piliavin et al. 1981, p. 144)

2.   Some supportive empirical evidence is to be found with respect to parents' attitudes toward the education of their children. Stevenson and Stigler (1992) note that "Schoolwork is considered to be the responsibility of teachers and students, rather than a major concern for parents" (p. 81) and "Each time a new need arises—whether it is how to behave in an earthquake or how to avoid dental plaque—Americans assume that the schools rather than the parents will respond to their children's need for information" (p. 83).

3.   In trying to understand this phenomenon, Mason (1994, p. 82) concludes that "These judges were citizens of their culture. They believed, as they were told by mass circulation magazines and child-rearing manuals, that mothers were more nurturing and morally superior to fathers and that children were best raised under their gentle guidance. They were willing, on a case by case basis, to award custody to mothers of young children, not as a woman's right, but for the sake of the child's nurture." This represents one possibility. Another might be an impulse to punish the errant husband. Yet another might be to offer a solution that supports both mother and child. Any of these—even in the smallest measure—would tip the judge's balance in favor of mothers, and, in the aggregate, lead to the extreme outcome.

4.   Schelling (1984) gives numerous compelling examples of intrapersonal preference changes. One can think of the enthusiasm and excitement that many parents feel while awaiting the birth of their child, and their optimism that they and their spouse will make the most delightful parents. These are probably most often heartfelt pronouncements, only to be replaced by equally heartfelt pronouncements of the demerits of their spouse as father/mother some number of years hence in difficult custody negotiations.

5.   Answers for our own time come from technological developments. Yet we are reminded that surrogate parenting is a very old institution.

6.   Elster (1989) has suggested that one possibility for ensuring children's well-being following divorce is to ask parents to specify, while they are still married, the eventual dispensation of any children should a divorce occur in the future. They would then be bound by their earlier commitments, and would be able to take into account the gains and losses likely to be entailed by divorce prior to that decision. While this is appealing on the grounds that parents are more likely to be reasonable toward the other parent during marriage than during divorce, they cannot hope to foresee the conditions that would hold at the time of divorce. Further, their preferences at the time of divorce, although they may be less appealing, are nonetheless important.

7.   There are, of course, other good reasons for regular visitation, principally to encourage the continuation of the relationship between the child and the noncustodial parent.

References

Abbott, Grace. 1938a. *The Child and the State. Volume I. Legal Status in the Family. Apprenticeship and Child Labor*. Chicago: University of Chicago Press.

Abbott, Grace. 1938b. *The Child and the State. Volume II. The Dependent and the Delinquent child. The Child of Unmarried Parents*. Chicago: University of Chicago Press.

Ames, Howard. 1891. *The Motives For, and a New System of Divorce*. Gottingen: The George-Augustus University.

Anthony, Susan B. and I. Harper. [1883–1900] 1973. Pp. 413–470 in Alice Rossi, ed., *The Feminist Papers: From Adams to deBeauvoir*. New York: Columbia University Press.

Ariès, Phillipe. 1962. *Centuries of Childhood: A Social History of Family Life*. New York: Alfred A. Knopf.

Armstrong, W. A. 1972. "A Note on the Household Structure of Mid-Nineteenth-Century York in Comparative Perspective." Pp. 205–214 in P. Laslett, ed., *Household and Family in Past Time*. Cambridge: Cambridge University Press.

Atkins, Susan and Brenda Hoggett. 1984. *Women and the Law*. Oxford: Basil Blackwell.

Backhouse, Constance B. 1981. *Shifting Patterns in Nineteenth Century Canadian Custody Law, Volume I*. Toronto, Ontario: Osgoode Society.

Backhouse, Constance B. 1987. "Nineteenth Century Judicial Attitudes toward Child Custody, Rape and Prostitution." Pp. 43–67 in S. Martin and K. Mahoney, eds., *Equality and Judicial Neutrality*. Toronto: Carswell.

Badinter, Elisabeth. 1981. *The Myth of Motherhood: An Historical View of the Maternal Instinct*. London: Souvenir Press.

Banks, J.A. and Olive Banks. 1964. *Feminism and Family Planning in Victorian England*. Liverpool: Liverpool University Press.

Barrie, J. M. [1911] 1950. *Peter Pan*. New York: Charles Scribner's Sons.

Becker, Gary S. 1981. *A Treatise on the Family*. Cambridge, MA: Harvard University Press.

Becker, Gary S. 1991. *A Treatise on the Family*, 2nd ed. Cambridge, MA: Harvard University Press.

Bernard, Jessie. 1974. *The Future of Motherhood*. New York: Dial Press.

Blackstone, William. [1765] 1979. *Commentaries on the Laws of England*. G. Sharwood, ed. 4 Vols. Chicago: University of Chicago Press.

Blakesley, Christopher. 1981. "Child Custody and Parental Authority in France, Louisiana and Other States of the United States: A Comparative Analysis." *Boston College International and Comparative Law Review* 4(2):283–359.

Bland, Lucy. 1987. "The Married Woman, the 'New Woman' and the Feminist: Sexual Politics of the 1890s." Pp. 141–164 in Jane Rendall, ed., *Equal or Different: Women's Politics 1800–1914*. Oxford: Basil Blackwell.

Bloch, Ruth H. 1978. "American Feminine Ideals in Transition: The Rise of the Moral Mother, 1785–1815." *Feminist Studies* 4(2):101–126.

Boris, Eileen and P. Bardaglio. 1983. "The Transformation of Patriarchy: The Historic Role of the State." Pp. 70–93 in I. Diamond, ed., *Families, Politics and Public Policy: A Feminist Dialogue on Women and the State*. New York: Longman.

Bose, Christine E. 1987. "Dual Spheres." Pp. 267–285 in Beth Hess and Uyra M. Ferree, eds., *Analyzing Gender: A Handbook of Social Science Research*. Newbury Park, CA: Sage.

Boyd, Susan B. 1989. "From Gender Specificity to Gender Neutrality: Ideologies in Canadian Custody Law." Pp. 126–157 in Carol Smart and Selma Sevenhuijsen, eds., *Child Custody and the Politics of Gender*. London: Routledge.

Bremner, Robert H. 1971. *Children and Youth in America: A Documentary History. Volume II: 1866–1932*. Cambridge, MA: Harvard University Press.

Briggs, A. 1961. "The Welfare State in Historical Perspective." *Archives Europeennes de Sociologie* 2(2):221–259.

Brophy, Julia. 1982. "Parental Rights and Children's Welfare: Some Problems of Feminists' Strategy in the 1920's." *International Journal of the Sociology of Law* 10:149–168.

Brophy, Julia and Carol Smart. 1981. "From Disregard to Disrepute: The Position of Women in Family Law." *Feminist Review* 9:3–16.

Buchanan, Allen E. 1991. "The Physician's Knowledge and the Patient's Best Interest." Pp. 93–112 in Edmund Pellegrino, ed., *Ethics, Trust, and the Professions: Philosophical and Cultural Aspects*. Washington, D.C.: Georgetown University Press.

Carrigan, Thomas C. [1911] 1974. "The Law and the American Child." Pp. 122–183 in Robert Bremner, Sanford Katz, Rachel Marks, and William Schmidt, eds., *Children and Youth: Social Problems and Social Policy. The Legal Rights of Children*. New York: Arno Press.

Chambers, David L. 1984. "Rethinking Substantive Rules for Custody Disputes in Divorce." *Michigan Law Review* 83:477–567.

Cherlin, Andrew J. 1981. *Marriage, Divorce, Remarriage*. Cambridge, MA: Harvard University Press.

Colcord, Joanna C. 1919. *Broken Homes: A Study of Family Desertion and Its Social Treatment*. New York: Russell Sage Foundation.

Coleman, James S. 1990. *Foundations of Social Theory*. Cambridge, MA: Harvard University Press.

Coleman, James S. 1993. "The Rational Reconstruction of Society: 1992 Presidential Address." *American Sociological Review* 58(1):1–15.

Conway, Jill K. 1982. *The Female Experience in Eighteenth and Nineteenth Century America: A Guide to the History of American Women*. New York: Garland Publishing.

Davin, Anna. 1978. "Imperialism and Motherhood." *History Workshop* 5:9–65.

Davis, Kingsley. 1944. "Sociological and Statistical Analysis." *Law and Contemporary Problems* 10(4):700–720.

Day, Clarence. 1932. *God and My Father*. New York: A.A. Knopf.

DeMause, Lloyd. 1974. *The History of Childhood*. New York: Psychohistory Press.

de Swaan, Abram. 1988. *In Care of the State: Health Care, Education and Welfare in Europe and the U.S.A. in the Modern Era*. New York: Oxford University Press.

Demo, David H. and Alan C. Acock. 1988. "The Impact of Divorce on Children." *Journal of Marriage and the Family* 50(3):619–648.

Demos, John. 1986. "The Changing Faces of Fatherhood." Pp. 41–67 in J. Demos, *Past, Present and Personal: The Family and the Lifecourse in American History*. New York: Oxford University Press.

Dohrnbusch, Sanford M., J. Merrill Carlsmith, Steven J. Bushwall, Phillip L. Ritter, Herbert Leiderman, Albert H. Hastorf, and Ruth T. Gross. 1985. "Single Parents, Extended Households, and the Control of Adolescents." *Child Development* 56(2):326–341.

Ehrenreich, Barbara and Deirdre English. 1978. *For Her Own Good: 150 Years of the Experts' Advice to Women*. Garden City, NY: Anchor Press.

Einhorn, Jay. 1986. "Child Custody in Historical Perspective: A Study of Changing Social Perceptions of Divorce and Child Custody in Anglo-American Law." *Behavioral Sciences and the Law* 4(2):119–135.

Elster, Jon. 1989. *Solomonic Judgments: Studies in the Limitations of Rationality*. Cambridge: Cambridge University Press.

Emerson, Richard. 1962. "Power-Dependence Relations." *American Sociological Review* 27(1):31–41.

Field, G. W. [1888] 1981. *The Legal Relations of Infants, Parent and Child, and Guardian and Ward: And a Particular Consideration of Guardianship in the State of New York*. Littleton, CO: Fred B. Rothman.

Fineman, Martha. 1989. "Custody Determination at Divorce: The Limits of Social Science Research and the Fallacy of the Liberal Ideology of Equality." *Canadian Journal of Women and the Law* 3(1):88–110.

Flora, Peter, Franz Kraus, and Winfried Pfenning. 1983. *State, Economy, and Society in Western Europe 1815–1975*. Volume I. *The Growth of Mass Democracies and Welfare States*. Volume II. *The Growth of Industrial Societies and Capitalist Economies*. Frankfurt: Campus Verlag.

Folberg, Jay. 1984. "Custody Overview." Pp. 3–15 in Jay Folberg, ed., *Joint Custody and Shared Parenting*. Washington, D.C.: Bureau of National Affairs.

Furstenberg, Frank F., Jr. and Andrew Cherlin. 1991. *Divided Families: What Happens to Children When Parents Part*. Cambridge, MA: Harvard University Press.

Garfinkel, Irwin. 1994. *Assuring Child Support: An Extension of Social Security*. New York: Russell Sage Foundation. In press.

Garfinkel, Irwin and Sara S. McLanahan. 1986. *Single Mothers and Their Children: A New American Dilemma*. Washington, D.C.: Urban Institute Press.

Glendon, Mary Ann. 1989. *The Transformation of Family Law: State, Law and Family in the United States and Western Europe*. Chicago: The University of Chicago Press.

Goldin, Claudia. 1990. *Understanding the Gender Gap: An Economic History of American Women*. New York: Oxford University Press.

Goldstein, Joseph, Anna Freud, and Albert J. Solnit. 1979a. *Before the Best Interests of the Child*. New York: Free Press.

Goldstein, Joseph, Anna Freud, and Albert J. Solnit. 1979b. *Beyond the Best Interests of the Child*. New York: Free Press.

Gordon, Linda and Sara McLanahan. 1991. "Single Parenthood in 1900." *Journal of Family History* 16(2):97–116.

Graveson, R.H. and F.R. Crane, eds. 1957. *A Century of Family Law 1857–1957*. London: Sweet and Maxwell.

Grossberg, Michael. 1983. "Who Gets the Child? Custody, Guardianship, and the Rise of a Judicial Patriarchy in Nineteenth Century America." *Feminist Studies* 9(2):235–260.

Grossberg, Michael. 1985. *Governing the Hearth: Law and Family in 19th Century America*. Chapel Hill: The University of North Carolina Press.

Hardin, Russell. 1982. *Collective Action*. Baltimore: The Johns Hopkins University Press.

Harris, Barbara J. 1978. *Beyond Her Sphere: Women and the Professions in American History*. Westport, CT: Greenwood Press.

Hechter, Michael. 1987. *Principles of Group Solidarity*. Berkeley: University of California Press.

Hechter, Michael, Debra Friedman, and Satoshi Kanazawa. 1992. "The Attainment of Global Order in Heterogeneous Societies." Pp. 79–97 in James S. Coleman and Thomas J. Fararo, eds., *Rational Choice Theory: Advocacy and Critique*. Newbury Park: Sage Publications.

Heimer, Carol. 1985. *Reactive Risk and Rational Action: Managing Moral Hazard in Insurance Contracts*. Berkeley: University of California Press.

Hess, Robert D. and Kathleen A. Camara. 1979. "Post-Divorce Family Relationships as Mediating Factors in the Consequences of Divorce for Children." *Journal of Social Issues* 35:79–96.

Hetherington, E. Mavis 1979. "Divorce: A Child's Perspective." *American Psychologist* 34:851–858.

Hetherington, E. Mavis, Martha Cox, and Roger Cox. 1978. "The Aftermath of Divorce." Pp. 149–176 in J. H. Stevens, Jr. and M. Mathews, eds., *Mother–child, Father–child Relations*. Washington, D.C.: National Association for the Education of Young Children.

Hetherington, E. Mavis, Martha Cox, and Roger Cox. 1979. "Play and Social Interaction in Children Following Divorce." *Journal of Social Issues* 35(4):26–49.

Hetherington, E. Mavis, Martha Cox, and Roger Fox. 1982. "Effects of Divorce on Parents and Children." Pp. 233–288 in M. E. Lamb, ed., *Nontraditional Families*. Hillsdale NJ: Erlbaum.

Hochheimer, Lewis. 1891. *The Law Relating to the Custody of Infants, Including Forms and Precedent*. Baltimore: Harold B. Scrimger.

Hollingsworth, T. H. 1957. "A Demographic Study of the British Ducal Families." *Population Studies* 11(1):4–26.

James, Henry. [1897] 1987. *What Maisie Knew*. Harmondsworth, England: Penguin Books.

Johnsen, Julia. 1925. *Selected Articles on Marriage and Divorce*. New York: H. W. Wilson.

Katz, Sanford, ed. 1974. *The Youngest Minority I: Lawyers in Defense of Children*. Chicago: American Bar Association.

Katz, Sanford, ed. 1977. *The Youngest Minority II: Lawyers in Defense of Children*. Chicago: American Bar Association.

Katz, Stanley N. 1979. "Introduction." Pp. iii–xiii in William Blackstone, *Commentaries on the Laws of England, Volume I.* Chicago: University of Chicago Press.

Kinard, E. Milling and Helen Reinherz. 1984. "Marital Disruption: Effects on Behavioral and emotional Functioning in Children." *Journal of Family Issues* 5(1):90–115.

Kinard, E. Milling and Helen Reinherz. 1986. "Effects of Marital Disruption on Children's School Aptitude and Achievement." *Journal of Marriage and the Family* 48(2):285–293.

Kurdek, Lawrence A. 1981. "An Integrative Perspective on Children's Divorce Adjustment." *American Psychologist* 36:856–866.

Kurdek, Lawrence A. and Albert E. Siesky, Jr. 1980. "Children's Perceptions of Their Parents' Divorce." *Journal of Divorce* 3(4):339–378.

Kurdek, Lawrence A., Darlene Blisk, and Albert E. Siesky, Jr. 1981. "Correlates of Children's Long-Term Adjustment to their Parents' Divorce." *Developmental Psychology* 17(5):565–579.

Lasch, Christopher. 1983. "The Family as a Haven in a Heartless World." Pp. 102–113 in Arlene S. Skolnick and Jerome H. Skolnick, eds., *Family in Transition: Rethinking Marriage, Sexuality, Child Rearing, and Family Organization.* 4th ed. Boston: Little, Brown.

Laslett, Peter. 1972. *Household and Family in Past Time: Comparative Studies in the Size and Structure of the Domestic Group over the Last Three Centuries in England, France, Serbia, Japan, and Colonial North America, with Further Materials from Western Europe.* Cambridge: Cambridge University Press.

Latane, Bibb and John Darley. 1969. "Bystander 'Apathy'." *American Scientist* 57:244–268.

Latane, Bibb and John Darley. 1976. *Help in a Crisis: Bystander Response to an Emergency.* Morristown, NJ: General Learning Press.

Latane, Bibb and Steve Nida. 1981. "Ten Years of Research on Group Size and Helping." *Psychological Bulletin* 89:308–324.

Latane, Bibb, Steve Nida, and D. Wilson. 1981. "The Effects of Group Size on Helping Behavior." Pp. 287–313 in J. P. Rushton and R. M. Sorentino, eds., *Altruism and Helping Behavior.* Hillsdale, NJ: Erlbaum.

Lichtenberger, James. [1931] 1972. *Divorce: A Social Interpretation.* New York: Arno Press.

Livermore, Mary A., Amelia E. Barr, Rose Terry Cooke, Elizabeth Stuart Phelps, and Jennie June. 1890. "Women's Views of Divorce." *North American Review* 150:110–135.

Lowe, Marian, ed. 1983. *Women's Nature: Rationalizations of Inequality.* New York: Pergamon Press.

Luker, Kristin. 1984. *Abortion and the Politics of Motherhood.* Berkeley: University of California Press.

Maccoby, Eleanor and Robert H. Mnookin. 1992. *Dividing the Child: Social and Legal Dilemmas of Custody.* Cambridge, MA: Harvard University Press.

Maidment, Susan. 1984. *Child Custody and Divorce: The Law in Social Context.* London: Croom Helm.

Margolis, Maxine L. 1984. *Mothers and Such: Views of American Women and Why They Changed.* Berkeley: University of California Press.

Mason, Mary Ann. 1991. "Motherhood v. Equal Treatment." *Journal of Family Law* 29(1):1–50.

Mason, Mary Ann. 1994. *From Father's Property to Children's Rights: A History of Child Custody in the United States.* New York: Columbia University Press.

Matthaei, Julie A. 1982. *An Economic History of Women in America: Women's Work, the Sexual Division of Labor, and the Development of Capitalism.* New York: Schocken Books.

McIlwraith, Malcolm. 1917. "Separation and Divorce." *Law Quarterly Review* 33:335–341.

McLanahan, Sara S. 1985. "Family Structure and the Reproduction of Poverty." *American Journal of Sociology* 90(4):873–901.

Mead, Margaret. 1932. "Contrasts and Comparisons from Primitive Society." Pp. 23–28 in Donald Young, ed., *The Modern American Family.* Annals of the American Academy of Political and Social Science, Vol. 160. Philadelphia.

Milnes, Monckton. [1858] 1975. *On the Property of Married Women and the Law of Divorce.* Buffalo, NY: Wm. S. Hein.

Minow, Martha and Richard Weissbourd. 1993. "Social Movements for Children." *Daedalus* 122(1):1–29.

Mitterauer, Michael and Reinhard Sieder. 1982. *The European Family: Patriarchy to Partnership from the Middle Ages to the Present.* Translated by K. Oosterveen and M. Horzinger. Chicago: University of Chicago Press.

Mnookin, Robert. 1975. "Child-Custody Adjudication: Judicial Functions in the Face of Indeterminacy." *Law and Contemporary Problems* 39(3):226–293.

Mnookin, Robert and D. Kelly Weisberg. 1989. *Child, Family and State: Problems and Materials on Children and the Law,* 2nd ed. Boston: Little, Brown.

Monroe, Day. 1932. *Chicago Families: A Study of Unpublished Census Data.* Chicago: University of Chicago Press.

O'Donovan, Katherine. 1979. *The Male Appendage: Legal Definitions of Women.* New York: St. Martin's.

O'Donovan, Katherine. 1985. *Sexual Divisions in Law.* London: Weidenfeld and Nicolson.

Ogus, A. I. 1982. "Great Britain," Pp. 150–264 in P. Kohler and H. Zacher, eds., *The Evolution of Social Insurance 1881–1981: Studies of Great Britain, France, Switzerland, Austria, and Germany.* London: Frances Pinter (Publishers).

Ostrom, Elinor. 1990. *Governing the Commons: The Evolution of Institutions for Collective Action.* Cambridge: Cambridge University Press.

Peterson, James L. and Nicholas Zill. 1986. "Marital Disruption, Parent-Child Relationships, and Behavior Problems in Children." *Journal of Marriage and the Family* 48(2):295–307.

Phillips, Roderick. 1988. *Putting Asunder: A History of Divorce in Western Society.* Cambridge: Cambridge University Press.

Piliavin, Jane A., John F. Dovidco, Samuel L. Gaertner, and Russell D. Clark, III. 1981. *Emergency Intervention.* New York: Academic Press.

Pomeroy, John Norton. 1892. *A Treatise on Equity Jurisprudence,* 3 vols., 2nd ed. San Franciso, CA: Bancroft-Whitney.

Preston, Samuel H. and Michael R. Haines. 1991. *Fatal Years: Child Mortality in Late Nineteenth Century America.* Princeton: Princeton University Press.

Proceedings of the Adjourned Meeting of the National Congress on Uniform Divorce Laws. 1906. Harrisburg, PA: Harrisburg Publishing Co.

Puxon, Margaret. [1922] 1971. *Family Law*. Harmondsworth, England: Penguin Books.

Radin, Norma. 1981. "The Role of the Father in Cognitive, Academic and Intellectual Development." Pp. 379–427 in Michael E. Lamb, ed., *The Role of the Father in Child Development*, 2nd ed. New York: Wiley.

Rajhadon, P. Anuman. 1965. "Customs Connected with Birth and the Rearing of Children." Pp. 115–204 in Donn V. Hart, P. Anuman Rajhadon, and Richard J. Coughlin, eds., *Southeast Asian Birth Customs*. New Haven: Yale University Press.

Regan, Milton C., Jr. 1993. *Family Law and the Pursuit of Intimacy*. New York: New York University Press.

Ringrose, Hyacinthe. 1911. *Marriage and Divorce Laws of the World*. London: The Masson-Draper Co.

Rothman, Sheila M. 1978. *Woman's Proper Place: A History of Changing Ideals and Practices, 1870 to the Present*. New York: Basic Books.

Royal Commission on Divorce and Matrimonial Causes: 1909. 1912–13 [Cd. 6478–82], v. 18–20.

Ryan, Mary P. 1981. *Cradle of the Middle Class: The Family in Oneida County, New York, 1790–1865*. Cambridge: Cambridge University Press.

Saint-Jours, Yves. 1982. "France," Pp. 93–149 in P. Kohler and H. Zacher, eds., *The Evolution of Social Insurance 1881–1981: Studies of Great Britain, France, Switzerland, Austria, and Germany*. London: Frances Pinter (Publishers).

Savage, Gail. 1983. "The Operation of the 1857 Divorce Act, 1860–1910: A Research Note." *Journal of Social History* 16:103–110.

Schelling, Thomas C. 1984. *Choice and Consequence*. Cambridge, MA: Harvard University Press.

Shinn, Marybeth. 1978. "Father Absence and Children's Cognitive Development." *Psychological Bulletin* 85(2):295–324.

Shorter, Edward. 1975. *The Making of the Modern Family*. New York: Basic Books.

Simmel, Georg. 1950. *The Sociology of Georg Simmel*. Translated, edited, and with an introduction by Kurt Wolff. Glencoe, IL: Free Press.

Skocpol, Theda. 1992. *Protecting Soldiers and Mothers: The Political Origins of Social Policy in the United States*. Cambridge, MA: The Belknap Press of Harvard University Press.

Smart, Carol. 1989. *Feminism and the Power of Law*. London: Routledge. Smart, Carol and Julia Brophy. 1985. "Locating Law: A Discussion of the Place of Law in Feminist Politics." Pp. 1–20 in J. Brophy and C. Smart, eds., *Women in Law: Explorations in Law, Family and Sexuality*. London: Routledge and Kegan Paul.

Solnit, Albert J. 1983. "Children's and Parent's Reactions to Divorce." *Psychiatric Hospital* 14(3):133–139.

Speth, Linda E. 1982. "The Married Women's Property Acts, 1839–1865: Reform, Reaction, or Revolution?" Pp. 69–91 in D. Kelly Weisberg, ed., *Women and the Law: The Social Historical Perspective*. Cambridge: Schenkman Publishing Co.

Stevenson, Harold W. and James W. Stigler. 1992. *The Learning Gap: Why Our Schools Are Failing and What We Can Learn from Japanese and Chinese Education.* New York: Summit Books.

Stone, Lawrence. 1979. *The Family, Sex and Marriage in England 1500–1800.* New York: Harper & Row.

Ursel, Jane. 1986. "The State and the Maintenance of Patriarchy: A Case Study of Family, Labour, and Welfare Legislation in Canada." Pp. 150–191 in J. Dickenson and B. Russell, eds., *Family, Economy and State: The Social Reproduction Process under Capitalism.* London: Croom Helm.

U.S. Bureau of the Census. *Historical Abstracts.* 1980. Washington, D.C.: Government Printing Office.

U.S. Bureau of the Census. *Special Reports. Marriage and Divorce, 1867–1906. Part I. Summary, Laws, Foreign Statistics. Part II. General Tables.* Washington, D.C.: Government Printing Office.

U.S. Bureau of the Census. [1978]. *Marriage and Divorce 1916, 1922–32.* Westport, CT: Greenwood Press.

United States Congressional Record. Proceedings on the Uniform Marriage and Divorce Act. Session 49 (1886–87) to Session 70 (1928). Volumes 18–69.

Vandepol, Ann. 1982. "Dependent Children, Child Custody, and the Mothers' Pensions: The Transformation of State-Family Relations in the Early 20th Century." *Social Problems* 29(3):221–235.

Wallerstein, Judith. 1983. "Children of Divorce: The Psychological Tasks of the Child." *American Journal of Orthopsychiatry* 53(2):230–243.

Wallerstein, Judith. 1984. "Children of Divorce: Preliminary Report of a Ten-Year Follow-Up of Young Children." *American Journal of Orthopsychiatry* 54(3):444–458.

Wallerstein, Judith. 1985. "Children of Divorce: Emerging Trends." *Psychiatric Clinics of North America.* 8(4):837–855.

Wallerstein, Judith S. and Joan B. Kelly. 1975. "The Effects of Parental Divorce: The Experiences of the Preschool Child." *Journal of the American Academy of Child Psychiatry* 14:600–616.

Wallerstein, Judith S. and Joan B. Kelly. 1976. "The Effects of Parental Divorce: Experiences of the Child in Later Latency." *American Journal of Orthopsychiatry* 46:256–269.

Wallerstein, Judith S. and Joan B. Kelly. 1980. *Surviving the Breakup: How Children and Parents Cope with Divorce.* New York: Basic Books.

Walton, Frederick. 1912. *Historical Introduction to the Roman Law.* Edinburgh: W. Green.

Weiss, Yoram and Robert J. Willis. 1985. "Children as Collective Goods and Divorce Settlements." *Journal of Labor Economics* 3(3):268–292.

Weitzman, Lenore J. 1985. *The Divorce Revolution: The Unexpected Social and Economic Consequences for Women and Children in America.* New York: Free Press.

Willcox, Walter Francis. [1891] 1969. *The Divorce Problem.* New York: AMS Press.

Wrigley, E. A. and R. S. Schofield. 1981. *The Population History of England 1541–1871: A Reconstruction.* London: Edward Arnold (Publishers) Ltd.

Zainaldin, Jamil S. 1979. "The Emergence of a Modern American Family Law: Child Custody, Adoption, and the Courts, 1796–1851." *Northwestern University Law Review* 73(6):1038–1089.

Index